LETTERS TO THE CONTEMPORARY CHURCH

J M Tucker
2005.

Tim Mark was a
controversial
mine at
Didsbury College
Bristol.

Letters to the Contemporary Church

LETTERS TO THE CONTEMPORARY CHURCH

Timothy Mark

TJM PUBLICATIONS
Doncaster
2005

Letters to the Contemporary Church

British Library Cataloguing in Publication Data

A record for this book is available from the British Library

ISBN 0-9538366-3-0

TJM Publications, Doncaster
www.tjmpublications.co.uk

Printed in Great Britain by
Ralph Wrightson Ltd, Earls Barton

To the Memory of

The Reverend Peter R Mark

Preacher, Teacher, Friend and Brother

Minister of the United Reformed Church

Penarth

Acknowledgements

Thanks to those members of the Churches in Sprotbrough, the Methodist Church and the Parish Church of St Mary's, who over the years have encouraged me to write these letters and for the interesting conversations that have ensued.

Permission to print these letters from the Editor of *The Church and Community in Sprotbrough* magazine is gratefully acknowledged. Clipart images are by courtesy of New Vision Technologies Inc., Canada.

Some of *The Letters* contain slight modifications to the original text. Thanks to my friend, Mrs Janice Wild, for her thorough reading of the manuscript and for her assistance in textual criticism. Thanks also to my friend, Mr Fred Bessant, whose several critical observations have enabled me (I hope!) to untangle some of the theological obscurities that he had uncovered.

Contents

Preface

Sprotbrough is a large village situated on the River Don to the west of Doncaster. In what is referred to as *the old village* there are two Christian congregations. St Mary's Parish Church has been at the centre of village life since the twelfth century. The Sprotbrough Methodist Church was built in 1938 but Methodists had been meeting nearby in an old Granary building since 1928. Both churches at present have strong thriving congregations.

Having been ordained in the Church of South India, Timothy is a Methodist Minister who holds the Bishop of Sheffield's licence to officiate at Anglican Services and over the years he has celebrated Holy Communion and preached regularly at both churches.

Letters to the Contemporary Church were first published in the local *Church and Community* Magazine[1] to which Timothy, along with others, has contributed the clergy letter regularly from 1982 to 2005. The forty-three letters cover a variety of themes, both pastoral and theological, but the author's keen desire to demonstrate the relevance and appeal of the Christian faith for modern twenty-first century people is apparent throughout. Timothy acknowledges three formative influences: Frederic Greeves who taught him theology at Bristol; John Robinson's *Honest to God* published in 1963 and the debate on secular theology that has continued ever since; and his life and ministry in the Church of South India.

This volume provides thought-provoking material and a valuable resource not only for teachers and preachers but for all those who are trying to understand the Christian Gospel in the context of modern, secular, multi-faith Britain.

---

[1] The title of the Magazine is **The Church and Community in Sprotbrough,** referred to throughout as **Church and Community.**

Foreword

I have known Timothy since 1977 when I became the Methodist Minister in Sprotbrough. It was an immense privilege to work with him and to be the Minister of his family.

It has been a heart-warming and mind-stretching experience to read these letters. It is clear that they have relevance far beyond the community for whom they were originally penned. They cover a wide range of topics, all of which are concerned with relating the Christian faith to everyday life.

Timothy is an evangelist, who whether he is reflecting on the Christmas story or discussing a political issue, communicates the gospel in the present tense using language that challenges his audience to think through the implications of Christian faith in the twenty-first century. Here is an invaluable resource for all people of faith and none.

These letters deserve the widest possible readership. It is my privilege to commend this book to the church and the world.

Keith Lackenby

Reverend Keith S Lackenby BA MMin Theol
Superintendent, Gainsborough Methodist Circuit and
Minister of Sprotbrough Methodist Church from 1977 to 1985

Christmas and New Year

Christmas: Light and Shadows

I wish you a happy and blessed Christmas. I am writing this on the day on which the first cruise missiles are reported to have arrived at Greenham Common.[2] Millions of people will celebrate Christmas on social security and unemployment benefit. Abroad, in India for example, millions will celebrate it hungry and with no jobs and no benefit. It would be pleasant, to say the least, if these hard political facts of 1983 could be forgotten or at least erased from our minds. A church newsletter must seem to some people to be the least appropriate place to draw attention to them. However, I make no apology because I believe that the Christian festival of Christmas is precisely about God's confrontation with the evil, suffering, madness and injustice of the world. Christmas means light shines in the darkness. Christmas means hope confronts despair. Christmas means God enters our bleeding, suffering world and triumphs over evil.

> *"Where misery cries out to thee*
> *The dark night wakes,*
> *Thy glory breaks*
> *And Christmas comes once more"*

---

[2] In 1981 a group of women, angered by the decision to site Cruise Missiles (guided nuclear missiles) in the UK, organised a protest march from Cardiff, Wales to Greenham Common Air Base near Newbury, Berkshire. Here they set up what became known as the Greenham Common Women's Peace Camp. Between 1981 and 1983 the protesters attempted to disrupt construction work at the base. Methods included blockading the base and cutting down parts of the fence. Cruise missiles were kept at the Greenham Common base from November 1983 as part of the Double Decision made by Nato in its response to the growing military might of the Soviet Union. They remained there until 1992 when they were removed under the terms of the US/Soviet Union Intermediate Nuclear forces (INF) agreement.

One of my favourite nativity paintings depicts Mary and the Christ child, with Joseph, shepherds and oxen standing by and looking towards the manger. A typical painting. Nothing remarkable, one might say. Suddenly one notices the very careful use of light and shadow. For the entire light in the picture emanates from the Christ child and is reflected in turn on the faces of his mother, then Joseph and the shepherds, then the oxen.[3] That simple painting describes in eloquent simplicity the meaning of Christmas; we can face Christ and reflect his light, or we can turn our backs upon him. If we turn our backs, we see the shadows of ourselves stretching out before us in alarming shapes and frightening distortions reflecting our egocentricity or our atheism. If we face him and join hands with others facing the light we see not only the light in the centre which is God but we see our fellow creatures all round the circle in the light of that central Love. An image of humanity? An image of the church? Perhaps it will do for both but in any case it is an excellent way of thinking about Christmas. It implies a requirement to look outwards beyond our immediate horizons and to respond to the needs of our fellow men with compassion and generosity. It also implies our need to look towards the Light and particularly towards Jesus Christ whose birth we celebrate, and in whom our lives find meaning and purpose.[4]

---

[3] See for example: Botticelli's **The Mystical Nativity** and Caravaggio's **Adoration of the Shepherds**
[4] First Published in **Church and Community**, December 1983

Responding To Christmas

Amidst the Christmas festivities, the Christingles, the nativity plays, the carol singing, the frantic sending and receiving of Christmas cards, the extra to eat and drink, the donations to Oxfam and Christian Aid, the excitement of wrapping and unwrapping gifts, the candles and services at church and chapel, the readings from Isaiah and the gospels, the meetings with old friends – there lurks the possibility for all of us, of real religious celebration.

But what sense do we really make of this story of the Christ child, of God incarnate, of divinity condescending into our humanity? Matthew's pretty story of the wise men and his ugly story of King Herod create feelings of incredulity perhaps, and also the recognition that two thousand years later it's still the poor who get the worst deal? Luke's charming description of angels, shepherds, swaddling clothes and a baby in a manger (it would spoil it to call it a cattle trough) evoke memories of our childhoods no doubt, and also the realisation that to propose that God enters the world somehow through poverty, requires some stretching of the imagination. Well, thankfully, the scholars tell us we do not have to take the details literally – it's all a poetic style, so to speak. The stories are rich *devotional* tales originating from the earliest days of the Christian community and we would be foolish to think that the details had any historical foundation. At heart, I like to kid myself that I am a twentieth century person; by not taking the details literally I am able to respond to the message emotionally, with both mind and heart.

Of course, we all respond to this Christmas event in our individual ways. Even if we are not overt churchgoers, we still respond to it. How can we possibly avoid it? Let me suggest three possible responses:

1. we can recognise its appeal to our common humanity and respond with an increased degree of compassion, charity, kindness, goodwill.

2. we can make a notional assent – (agreement) to the religious celebration, perhaps by uttering the odd prayer, or making an uncharacteristic appearance at a church service, or even – (threatening our natural agnosticism), allowing ourselves to ponder the possibility that it might be true.

3. we can listen to the sound of the angels and allow God to speak to us. But let me remind you, that real assents – are the hardest to make – they involve struggle, commitment, action, even a perilous substratum of doubt. The real assent involves a departure from *religion as dull habit* to a *religion as acute fever*. And if we catch that, what happens to twentieth century men and women then?[5]

---

[5] First Published in **Church and Community**, January 1990

Secular Christmas

I went to two special services at St Mary's over Christmas. On Christmas Eve I squeezed with Lorna, Kathryn and Richard[6] into a packed building to share in a Crib Service. There was the delight of singing carols by candle-light with eerie shadows on the walls, the excited sounds of children's voices, the familiar Scripture Readings and the procession to the Crib. There was also the comforting feeling of community, engendered by the presence of so many friends and neighbours, Anglicans, Methodists and others too who for all sorts of reasons are unable to attend Church week by week. Then early morning on Christmas Day I attended my second service and shared in the celebration of the Eucharist with twenty or so communicants. The contrast could not have been greater. On Christmas Eve the Church was packed; a few hours later at early Communion only a handful of people was present. The Crib Service is now possibly the most popular service in the village.[7] But early morning Communion clearly does not attract the crowds.[8] I have been wondering why this is so, and here are a few of my reflections.

---

[6] My wife, daughter and son
[7] So popular indeed that the Rector now arranges three Crib Services on Christmas Eve.
[8] There were barely half a dozen of us at a Methodist early Sunday morning Communion Service recently.

First, the Church fulfils a *social function*. It exists not only for the committed, but also for the lapsed, the uncertain, the perplexed, the agnostic, and even for the atheist. The church fulfils a need for everyone in the village whether they are Christian believers or not; it is the cement that binds the fabric of community and society together. One has no right and certainly no desire to label people but might it be the case that some of us present at the Crib Service would describe ourselves as perplexed about Christian doctrine, uncertain about moral values, and even agnostic regarding the reality of God? Hence, if we feel like that, our presence in a great crowd of worshippers would not seem threatening. Indeed it might even feel enjoyable, pleasant, and worthwhile. And rightly so, for in that service we were not only worshipping God but also celebrating our sense of common brotherhood and goodwill within our village community.

Second, the Church fulfils, and more obviously so, a *religious function* Holy Communion amongst other services reminds us of our fellowship with God. It also demands, I believe, not only a commitment to God and to each other, but also a willingness to think and behave theologically. So on Christmas morning, in the context of Holy Communion, the congregation faced the intellectual question of what it means to believe, to have faith, to live a life totally committed to God.[9] And the answer to that question is that faith always precedes understanding. Faith comes first, and then only because we have faith do we begin to discover the meaning of God working and living in our lives.

---

[9] My Christmas morning Sermon, 25 December 1998

Third, I have written as though the two functions were separate and different. But this is not so. The religious function of the Church embraces and includes its social function. I have written too as though the needs of the people at the two congregations at Christmas were different when in fact they are the same. Whether we describe ourselves as agnostic or believer is not the main point. Whether we attend Church regularly or just now and again is not the point. What is important is this. All of us belong to each other in this village. And God calls all of us not because we are good, or because we understand, or even because we have faith – but because he first loves us, and gives himself to us, in Jesus Christ.[10]

---

[10] First Published in *Church and Community*, February 1999

Christmas in Our Secular Community

There is something magical and exciting about the dark evenings leading up to Christmas. The shops and streets are full of bright lights and decorations. Carols are piped into the French Gate Centre[11] as we mortals scurry from shop to shop buying last minute presents and provisions. Each of us is trapped into a social ritual conditioned by the expectations of family and friends. We lament the commercialisation of Christmas, yet seem powerless to prevent it and incapable of resisting it. "I hate Christmas" said a woman teacher to me yesterday. We may not entirely agree with her, but we can sympathise with her sentiments of disliking four days of enforced entertaining, planning and cooking meals for a family suddenly enlarged by the descent of distant relatives.

On the other hand, to be frank, many of us will enjoy the extra food and drink, and will value the renewed contact with old friends which the flood of Christmas greetings will bring. And even the least generous amongst us will spare some thought and money for the poor and needy in our country and beyond. Christmas offers us a well deserved break; let us enjoy it.

But what of the Christmas story itself? What relevance has this tale of shepherds and angels, of wise men and a star, of a baby born in a

---

[11] This is a large shopping mall in the centre of Doncaster

10

cattle stall, for modern, secular, twentieth century man? Well, it can be interpreted in many ways. Some will say it's simply "make-believe" – as though make-believe is childish and unimportant. Others will tell you that "it's a myth" by which they mean no sensible person could possibly believe it to be true. Yet others will say, "it's just history" by which they mean it is remote and irrelevant. Others will describe it as nonsensical rubbish unworthy of the attention of intelligent people.

But could it be true – really true, in the sense that the story contains a significant message for unbelieving secular Sprotbrough man? Could it be true, that "the light shines in the darkness" for you, for me? Could it be true that "God was in Christ reconciling the world unto himself"? Could it be true, that the first century Jesus of Nazareth somehow shows us what God is like? Could the story of Jesus have a relevance and importance for our lives that matches and surpasses all the discoveries of enlightened, scientific, secular, twentieth century man? To say "yes" to these questions is not to descry the importance of a secular understanding of our world, but to recognise that truth is multi-dimensional, and that it is reasonable to hold both a scientific and a religious understanding of man. Perhaps the Christmas story has a meaning even for the most secular amongst us?

"Remember only one thing," said Badger, "the stories people tell have a way of taking care of them. If stories come to you, care for them. And learn to give them away where they are needed. Sometimes a person needs a story more than food to stay alive, that is why we put these stories into each other's memory". [12]

---

[12] Lopez Barry: **Crow and Weasel**, Ebury Press, 1991

Christmas church services are advertised elsewhere in this magazine. If you are not a regular visitor to Church, please accept from me a personal invitation to come to our services. You are most welcome, and whatever your personal beliefs, you are invited to be present. Christian believers find that Christmas is a special opportunity to renew their faith in God, in the God "who becomes man and dwells among us full of grace and truth". But for all of us, including the most secular amongst us, church services can provide an opportunity for quiet reflection, and for sharing and demonstrating that we all belong to a community of peace, brotherhood and goodwill.[13]

---

[13] First Published in *Church and Community*, December 1991

An Impromptu Sermon

I am writing this on the second Sunday after the Epiphany. The lessons I read in Church this morning provoked an impromptu sermon. The first lesson, from the Book of Samuel, describes the young Samuel's call from God and his ultimate response: "Speak, Lord, your servant hears". The second is an extract of Paul's defence before King Agrippa in which he relates his call on the Damascus road, ending with that memorable statement: "And so, King Agrippa, I did not disobey the heavenly vision". The third reading, from St John's Gospel, describes the cynical and sceptical Nathanael's encounter with Jesus and his confession "Rabbi, you are the son of God". Now impromptu sermons should either not be given at all, or at least they must be very short. Well, mine was very short. I referred to that word we use so often in church, "grace", and how according to that eminent twentieth century theologian, Karl Barth, none of us would be able to utter the word God, or even conceive of the existence of God, were it not for God revealing himself to us. Being called by God is to respond to an initiative that is entirely God's. Or as today's collect puts the matter so succinctly:

Almighty God, by whose grace alone we are accepted and called to your service; strengthen us by your Holy Spirit and make us worthy of our calling; through Jesus Christ our Lord.

Having been called by God, what does it mean today to say: "Speak, Lord, thy servant hears"? We live in a very different world from that of Samuel, or Paul, or the first disciples. We live in a secular society where the majority of people does not take religion and the possibility of divine encounter seriously. We are linked together also in one huge inter-global network of communications, what some have described as the secular city. Our neighbours are no longer just those next door, or even those 50 miles away; we can communicate in seconds by telephone, or computer, or fax, or satellite to people all round the world. What does it mean for us, therefore, to respond to the call of God?

Let me suggest three clues: the first from today's Bible readings – we begin the life of faith through God's grace alone. The second is to recognise that witness in a secular city might mean changing some of our traditional ways of doing things in church and of adventuring out into unexplored, even hostile territory. The third is to realise that Christians belong to two places; they are always pilgrims, strangers and foreigners, who can never be totally at home "in the old dispensation",[14] who are travelling towards a city[15] "by whose light the nations shall walk", and where "the kings of the earth shall bring into it all their splendour".[16] [17]

---

[14] T S Eliot, "Journey of the Magi", **Collected Poems 1909-1935**, Faber, 1958.
[15] Revelation Chapter 21, verses 22-26.
[16] Revelation Chapter 21, verse 24.
[17] First Published in **Church and Community**, February 1996

How Can We Bridge The Gap?

I mean, how can that story of Jesus, of angels, shepherds, wise men, have relevance for twenty-first century man? How can I make that leap of faith that makes the story of the carpenter of Nazareth who lived 2000 years ago, a story that has meaning for me? Is it really true? Is it so true that if I believe it the very foundation of my life will be shaken? I guess that it is possible that you and I know the Christmas story so well, so intimately, that it ceases to make any impact upon us?

Some years ago a Methodist Minister friend and I were engaged in theological discussion. Actually we were talking about a Nativity Service that he had been arranging in his church. He explained that the person in charge of the service had insisted that there was no need to have the Gospel lesson read "because they all know the story." My friend insisted, "they might think they know it, but of course they don't!"

He had a point because the story is so remote, so quaint, so unusual and so unbelievable that it requires a big leap of faith to find any meaning in it at all. Most of us can probably recite the main events of the Christmas story but it is likely that, if we are absolutely honest, we find it very hard indeed to believe. If that is the case, it follows that most of our carol singing this Christmas will have been accompanied by a large dose of what the theologians call "de-myth-ologising", that is, translating the richly devotional tales of Christmas[18] into thought forms that are appropriate to modern, secular, Christian man in the twenty-first century.

One of the classic documents from antiquity is by an unknown writer, perhaps written in the second century between 130 to 150 AD, entitled the Letter to Diognetus. Here is an extract:

> *"Christians are not distinguished from the rest of mankind; either in locality or in speech or in customs. For they dwell not somewhere in cities of their own, neither do they use some different language, nor practise an extraordinary kind of life.... They dwell in their own countries but only as sojourners; they bear their share in all things as citizens, and they endure all hardships as strangers. Every foreign country is a fatherland to them, and every fatherland is foreign... So Christians have their abode in the world, and yet they are not of the world."* [19]

The German theologian Bonhoeffer wrote:

> *"To be a Christian does not mean to be religious in a particular way. It is not the religious act that makes the Christian, but participation in the sufferings of God in secular life. It means participation in the powerlessness of God in the world."* [20]

Christmas is actually a story for our day. It is about poverty, powerlessness and politics. This means that in the midst of our secular, ordinary everyday life we can find God. God is not remote from us! We find him specifically amongst those who are suffering and amongst those who have no-one to speak for them – the disadvantaged, the poor, the hungry and refugees. In theological language, we say *it is*

---

[18] Richardson Alan: **An Introduction to the Theology of the New Testament**, SCM Press 1958, page 173.
[19] Gwatkin H M: **Selections from Early Christian Writers**, Macmillan 1920, page 13 ff
[20] Bonhoeffer D: **Letters and Papers from Prison**, Macmillan 1967

about the possibility of finding the divine in the midst of the secular. A most eloquent sign of his presence is the birth of Jesus.[21] More eloquent still is his execution on the cross. God is the God who meets us at the point of utter weakness, powerlessness, and hopelessness. "Come down from the cross!" they mocked. But he won't come down. He hangs there and dies. In poverty, weakness, and utter desolation he meets us. To follow him, is to meet him, precisely there. I suspect that if not poverty, certainly weakness and desolation are themes with which we can identify? That I believe is the heart of the Christmas story.[22]

---

[21] See **Isaiah** Chapter 7 verse 14
[22] First Published in ***Church and Community***, February 2001

Watch Night Service in India

In the watch night service in St Peter's Church, Thanjavur, South India, there is a beautiful tradition. The Presbyter's sermon spans the magic hour of midnight. He begins with a backward look at the year which is passing and concludes with a forward look to the New Year just beginning. At the stroke of midnight there is a break in the sermon, silence and corporate prayer. There is a great value in that Indian tradition, and we might choose to emulate it – beginning the year on our knees, awake, sober, reflective and receptive to God's grace.

A friend of mine has recently published a book called *The Christian Juggler*[23]. With reference to the traditional pattern of church life that many of us know, love and cherish, he writes: "It has kept us safe but stale, coherent but enclosed, faithful but deaf, loyal but not loving". Bryan Rippin is a Methodist Minister writing as Church leader. Yet he courageously implies that the Church might be stale, inward-looking and deaf to the needs of others. He writes for "dancers not dogmatists." In saying this he invites us to be creative in our thinking and to take risks in our theology. He pleads for a quality of Christian life which emphasises "exploration," "humanity" and "solidarity". These are strong words which require careful thought. They present an image of the church that risks its future by standing alongside the

---

[23] Rippin Bryan: **The Christian Juggler**, Epworth, 1985

poor, the deprived, the maimed and the helpless, irrespective of their creed, colour or circumstance. It reminds us of the need to be aware of the lonely in the midst of the crowd, and of the stranger on our doorstep crying out to be a neighbour. It reminds us too of our solidarity with the third world and for all who are striving for basic human rights, for example – in El Salvador, in South Africa and in the Sudan.

It is good to be at the beginning of a New Year. As we say farewell to 1986 we have many things to thank God for. There are also some regrets, sadness, and unfulfilled dreams. There are things to forget, and forgiveness to ask. But let our minds concentrate on the good things which have happened to us; and let us thank God for them. The New Year is a time of promise and hope. For Christians, this hope is grounded in our understanding and experience of the life, death and resurrection of Jesus Christ. Our lives are encompassed by the goodness and love of God: that remains true, whether we perceive it or not. Whatever our circumstances, therefore, let us believe in the reality and goodness of God. And holding fast to that conviction let each of us step boldly into the New Year – in faith, in hope and with love.[24]

---

[24] First Published in ***Church and Community***, January 1987

Epiphany

I enjoy writing my occasional contribution to this magazine because it provides me with an opportunity to communicate theological ideas. Moreover, I have the privilege of writing as one who is not beset by the constant pressures of circuit and parish, and whose lack of day-to-day involvement provides, therefore, the possibility of a somewhat detached perspective.   There is one difficulty, however, of which I am constantly aware, namely, that I have very little conception of the success of this enterprise.   I truly have no idea whether I succeed in communicating theological ideas!   I am told that communication includes three things: a sender, a message, and a receiver.   I have control over the first two, yes certainly, but I have very little understanding of the third.   It would be interesting to know whether people, reading my letters, are provoked or moved by my ideas!

I am writing this in Epiphany, the season when the Church celebrates the communication of its message far beyond the boundaries of Judaism, to those of other religious persuasions or none.   "Wise men came from the East...." foreigners no doubt, gentiles most certainly. The gospel of Christ has a universal dimension; the good news is for all men, in all places and at all times.   But this creates a problem for the Church.   How can it communicate this message whilst at the same time respecting the serious views and convictions of non-believers?   How can the Church communicate the gospel effectively in the midst of middle class, pleasure-seeking, affluent Sprotbrough?

In my Christmas Day sermon last month at St Mary's I made a serious attempt to address this issue.   I dared to suggest that the Christian significance of the Christmas festival was not about giving toys and gifts and having fun, but rather about facing the deeply personal, and frightening possibility of God meeting us at the centre of our lives. There are friends of mine who have faced intense personal tragedy and suffering in recent months and yet who have found God meeting them in their situation and being alongside them in their ordeal. "Finding God alongside us in our ordeal, at the depth of our being". Yes, that is what Christmas is really all about.

> *No ear shall hear his coming; but in this world of sin, where meek souls will receive him still, the dear Christ enters in.*

My point was, of course, not that one should not have fun, or give presents, or eat good food, but that this secular event should not be confused with the religious one.   On the other hand, if indeed the message, which the church has to communicate, is for all men, then the church's activities should reflect this.   In this sense, a church exists not only for the committed, but also for the lapsed, the uncertain, the perplexed, the agnostic, and even for the atheist.[25]   If we follow this argument one step further, one could say that the most important function of the church is its social one, that is, it is a unifying factor which brings together all members of society in a particular place.

---

[25] I am following here some ideas suggested by Peter Mullen "Why be good when God is money?", **The Guardian**, 31 Dec 94

So perhaps after all, the religious and the secular should go hand in hand, and my attempt on Christmas morning to suggest that they should be considered separately was misconstrued. But I will not concede my argument so easily. I agree that the church indeed has a social function, but its most important task, is to communicate with utmost conviction its belief that:

> *"God who at sundry times and in divers manners spake in time past unto the fathers by the prophets, hath in these last days spoken unto us by his Son..."*.[26] [27]

---

[26]**Letter to the Hebrews,** Chapter 1, verses 1 and 2 (Authorised Version).
[27] First Published in *Church and Community*, February 1995

New Year

May I take this opportunity to wish you a happy and joyful new year! I hope you have had a good Christmas and that in the midst of the frenzy of shopping and entertaining you have found some time to reflect on the meaning of the coming of Christ into the world. The message of the Christ Child in the manger bed is that God comes into the world to meet us at the place where we need him most. The truth is that each of us has different needs, and God enters our lives (if we will allow him to) and gives us the strength, solace, power, peace and healing that we need.

I remember speaking at a watch night service in India.[28] The intention was to review the old year and to look forward into the new. The message I gave then is one which I wish to share with you now. It is simple but also radically profound. It is the words of St. Paul: "His grace is sufficient for you". I believe this to be true. Can you, with me, look back over 1988 with all its delights, joys and pleasures, and all its difficulties, problems, anxieties too, and say that God's grace has been sufficient for you? I expect you can. Can you say it also if you have experienced suffering and grief? I expect you can. Can you say it too about your various relationships (some easy and some hard)? I expect you can. As we stand at the threshold of a New Year we can say with gratitude that God's grace has been sufficient to meet our

---

[28] See Letter *Watchnight Service in India*

need. What was true for 1988 will be so for 1989. Whatever happens in this coming year, God's grace is sufficient for all that we shall experience. The past, present and future are in his hands. Believe that, and face 1989 with trust and confidence "My grace is sufficient .... for you".

I cannot imagine all the situations of those who are kind enough to read these words. I am sure, however, that some of you will be facing the New Year with perhaps a measure of anxiety and fear. Whoever you are, and in whatever your circumstances, please find a moment this New Year's Eve, to kneel before the God who creates and redeems us, to commit your life to him. That is both the beginning of faith and its end.[29]

> By thy unerring Spirit led,
> We shall not in the desert stray;
> We shall not full direction need,
> Nor miss our providential way;
> As far from danger as from fear
> While love, almighty love is near[30]

---

[29] First Published in **Church and Community**, January 1989
[30] Charles Wesley: *Captain of Israel's host, and Guide*, **Hymns and Psalms**, Methodist Publishing House, London, 1983, No 62

Millennium

It was hot and humid. I could not sleep. I woke at four and tiptoed downstairs to make a drink and read. I read two thought-provoking articles from the current issue of *Theology* and one of them[31] by Timothy Jenkins[32] I discuss below. Let me share with you the gist of what Jenkins is saying in the hope that my attempt at précis will be found provocative by my readers too.

The question that Jenkins addresses is how are we to interpret the millennial event? What is special about December 31st 1999? Clearly, at one level it is no different from any other end of year, or indeed any other transition from one date to another. Most certainly, however, it is special for it marks two thousand years since the birth of Jesus Christ. Actually, the notion of measuring time from the birth of Jesus results from a proposal made by a sixth century monk, and this system of dating was agreed in this country at the Synod of Whitby in 664. Jenkins refers to the first millennium when the approach of the year 1000 was awaited with some anxiety. For example, the millennium is specifically referred to in the twentieth chapter of the *Book of Revelation*. It was not surprising, therefore, that an earthquake in the year 1000 gave rise to panic on a huge scale. There was "a preoccupation with predictive prophecy and date fixing,

---

[31] Timothy Jenkins: "An approach to the Millennium", **Theology**, May/June 1999, pages 161-169
[32] Jenkins is Dean of Jesus College, Cambridge.

flights into irrationality and libertinism, sectarian behaviour and fundamentalism".[33]   Very few people nowadays, points out Jenkins, expect the coming of Christ in the year 2000. He points out ironically how sophisticated we have now become, yet there has been talk of aeroplanes falling out of the sky, stockpiling of food, chaos on the international stock markets and "all of this apocalyptic speculation" fuelled by interested parties: "politicians, computer experts, bankers and journalists".[34]

So returning to his main point Jenkins re-phrases his question. If the millennium is more than a mere movement of chronological time from one moment to the next, then what is it exactly? The millennium raises the question, he says, of two thousand years of what? He writes: "It gives us that queasy feeling that our world of meaning, our order of common sense, our horizon, may be less natural, self-evident and assured than we normally assume".[35]

So the millennium marks the need for an interpretation that provides a view of human history and helps "make sense of things". It could point to a way of imagining how things could be different from what they are. It will respond hopefully to the demands and possibilities of the moment. It could create a vision of how human power and human will may be articulated in "a structure of trust", in a series of commitments under God "that might allow human nature, human

---

[33] Jenkins, op cit, page 163
[34] Ibid
[35] Ibid.page 165

flourishing and divine order to be joined together".[36] Jenkins sees the Church, and specifically Anglicanism, as providing the vision that we need, "a social vision of human flourishing" but within "a theological vision of who God is, and what he has done for us".[37]

So how will you approach the millennium? Where will you be at midnight on December 31st? What will be the Church's interpretation? I know that its message will be unequivocal and clear, inviting women and men to put their trust in God, to follow Christ into the twenty-first century, not looking backwards like Lot's wife, but pressing forwards in hope and confidence to build a better world where peace and justice prevail. At midnight, at the start of the millennium, we should be on our knees, or at least like those wise virgins, we should be awake.[38]

---

[36] Ibid, page 167
[37] Ibid, page 169
[38] First Published in *Church and Community*, August 1999

The Christian Church

The Old House

Just two miles away from Sprotbrough there is an old dilapidated house. I must have passed it hundreds of times but I had never noticed it until today. As I cycled towards it, I counted its nine chimneys and then stopped to stare at it. Broken pillars frame its old front door. All the windows are boarded up. The structure of the building is too unsafe to enter. The rooms that once echoed to the sounds of children's laughter are hidden from view. Iron gates guard the bare empty front garden where scented flowers once bloomed in abundance. Soon the ruin will be demolished and a new modern edifice will take its place; the social history locked inside the old building will disappear for ever.

In this picture of the old house being replaced by the new I perceive an image of the Christian Church. In both churches in this village building alterations are in process. The shape and facilities of the old are being replaced by the new. The necessary changes in the buildings are designed to enable the churches to respond more effectively to the needs of today. I suggest, however, that additional changes are now required, namely, in our understanding of what the Church[39] is supposed to be – what is its nature, what is its purpose, what should be its chief aim?

---

[39] I use the term "Church" to refer to the universal church of which Anglicans and Methodists are just a very small part.

It is now reported[40] that Anglicans and Methodists are to explore proposals for a "visibly united church" having just completed more than two years of informal talks.   During the next twelve months both churches will discuss a plan for closer integration before it is debated in the Church of England's General Synod in November 1997 and in the Methodist Conference.   Both churches have tried to unite before[41] and some envisage that a problematic issue in the present negotiations will be the question of the position of women bishops.   The unity consultation document, just published, proposes the aim of a visibly united church that would include a common profession of the one apostolic faith, recognising each other's baptism service and Eucharist, and a common jurisdiction by bishops over ministers.   The aim is closer integration rather than merger.

The Church of South India was created in 1947 by a union of four traditions: Anglican, Methodist, Congregationalist and Presbyterian. It was the first successful union of episcopal and non-episcopal ordered churches.   The Deed of Union included a *30 year period* during which the new united church would reflect on what changes needed to be made in its practice of ministry.   Another assurance was *The Pledge* whereby it was agreed that no congregation would have a tradition forced upon it against its will.

---

[40] This information is taken from a report in **The Guardian,** 10 July 96
[41] In 1972 and 1982

The Old House

When I came to live in Sprotbrough in 1975 I expected that by the time our children had grown up the two congregations would have grown much closer together than in fact has proved to be the case. Is it too much to hope that in the light of negotiations now starting again at national level, the local churches in Sprotbrough may consider becoming a Local Ecumenical Partnership?[42]

So back to the old house! In a hundred years' time, I am sure that much of our life together today as separate churches will be viewed with curiosity, even amusement. Our social history, apart from records in old registers, will be lost from view. The structure of the Christian Church as we know it now will have been replaced by new forms of Christian structure, worship and organisation. I have no doubt that the Bible will continue to be the foundation stone around which the life, witness and worship of the Church will be built. I guess too that Cranmer and Wesley will still be treasured as part of the catholic heritage of the Church. But back to the present, there is a job for us to do now, "to serve the present age, our calling to fulfil".[43]
[44]

---

[42] A *Local Ecumenical Partnership* is defined as existing "where there is a formal written agreement affecting the ministry, congregational life, buildings, and/or mission projects of more than one denomination; and a recognition of that agreement by the sponsoring body and by the appropriate denominational authorities". In the year 2000 a *Covenant Agreement* was entered into but at the time of this publication a *Local Ecumenical Partnership* had not been established.
[43] Charles Wesley: *A Charge to keep I have*, **Hymns and Psalms**, Methodist Publishing House, London, 1983, No 785
[44] First Published in **Church and Community** August 1996

Church Structures

How relevant are our church structures in Sprotbrough for the needs of the present time? By "structures" I mean not only the manner and content of our various worship services, but also the methods by which we organize our churches and the ways in which we approach the business of mission. Many of the visible signs of the church in Sprotbrough could be changed (even discarded) without compromising the essential meaning of "Church". For example, the long queues of cars along the Park on a Sunday morning, the actual times of worship, the clergy, or even our splendid buildings made sacred by the worship and prayers of generations before us. None of these structures is essential to the being of the church; they belong to what theologians have called *the bene esse*, that is, to the possible good of the church in contrast to *the esse* – the central core and basis of the life of the church. What then is this *esse* of the church? What aspects of the church are so essential that to deny them would be to deny its very existence? The answer, as I am sure all good Methodists and Anglicans know well, is that two things (or structures) belong to the *esse* of the church – worship (including the sacraments) and ministry. Yet it is also true that each of these can be expressed in a variety of ways. For example, house fellowships and home Eucharists can become the norm rather than the exception, and the full-time ordained ministry can be supplemented by a number of worker presbyters in full-time

34

secular employment, thus imposing little strain on the finances of the church.

Having lived in this village for seven years, I hope I may be forgiven if I spell out at least three implications, as I see them, of a hard and critical look at our church structures?

(1) In the post-covenant situation[45] in which we find ourselves, henceforth our planning and use of resources should be conducted as a joint exercise. We shall of course remain loyal and sensitive to our respective church traditions whilst working actively towards a visible united church in Sprotbrough under a "shared ministry" agreement.

(2) Ministry in its many forms must be recognised to be largely the function of the laity. (I am sure we have long ago discounted those three erroneous ideas of church leadership - that a priest is better than a layman, that a man is better than a woman, and that an adult is more important that a child). This means that many of us need to accept some specific pastoral responsibility for the community and neighbourhood in which we live.

(3) The ministry of the church has dimensions that stretch beyond the geographical boundaries of the village. Our responsibilities with the whole church for continuing mission and service to society, both in this country and in the third world, need to be kept constantly under

---

[45] This is a reference to the failed Anglican-Methodist unity proposals in 1982 which had been approved by the Methodist Conference but which failed to gain sufficient majorities in the Church of England Synod. It is pleasing to note that The Anglican and Methodist Churches signed a covenant in October 2003 committing themselves to "a common life of worship and mission in the years to come".

review. "The church exists for mission as fire exists for burning". The relevance of our church life must be judged, in the end, by our faithfulness to God's mission in the world. It is God's mission, not ours. Our part is summed up appropriately in the words of the controlling lesson for Advent Sunday:

> *"Therefore my people shall know my name: therefore they shall know in that day that I am he that doth speak: behold it is I."*
> *(Isaiah 52, verse 6).*[46]

---

[46] First Published in ***Church and Community***, November 1982

Not a Church Going Christian

"I'm a Christian" my friend said, "but not a church-going Christian".

"There must be many like that in Sprotbrough", I said.

"I was born in Sprotbrough" my friend said, "I played in the fields as a lad".

"And what use is the church then?" I said.

"The church should be there when you need it," my friend said.

My friend's opinions are probably echoed by many in this village for if all who live here attended the church services there just would not be enough room for us all. On the other hand, many folk just drop in now and again, for the odd christening, or a wedding, or a funeral – or just simply to sit down and be quiet for a moment.

My friend is absolutely right not to identify Christianity with church-going, although on the other hand it would be hard to imagine Christianity surviving without churches, or something similar to take their place. My friend is right, too (or up to a point anyway) when he says that the church should be there when you need it. For as the Rector of Sprotbrough has said to me on more than one occasion – "the church (by which he means the parish church community) belongs to everyone in the village".[47] Belonging in that sense means belonging because we live here. It's true also that the church (in its

---

[47] In conversation with the Reverend Canon Stuart Matthews, *Rector of Sprotbrough* from 1982 to 2000

widest sense) God's church (Methodists, Anglicans, Roman Catholics, Pentecostalists and all the others) belongs to all of us for it represents God himself in our midst. So it's correct to say that the church should be there when you need it; but of course, somebody or some people have got to be prepared to look after its upkeep, to keep it going as it were!

What did my friend mean when he said "when you need it"? I shall have to guess because he didn't tell me. I guess, however, that he means that we all need it at some time or another, particularly when some unexpected personal crisis occurs. Perhaps we need to be quiet. Maybe we need to be alone for a bit. Possibly we need to have a realistic confidential talk with someone. Yes, at some time or another we need to sort ourselves out – and going into a church might help a bit.

But I would like to pursue my friend's ideas a bit further and say that religion (for that's what going to church means) is only a stepping stone towards God. However moving, dynamic, exciting, thought provoking our religious services are, it is quite wrong to assume that they are to be identified with God. Churches, chapels, religion – provide one kind of setting where God can disclose himself to us. We should never forget, however, that they provide only the context, the possibility of God encountering us. Religion, and churches, provide the opportunity sometimes "to touch the hem of the transcendent". Well, come to think of it, it's not really churches that we need after all!

It's God whom we need. When we realise our need of God, that is probably when we feel the need to go to church.

One final thought – my old Principal, the Revd Dr Frederic Greeves, used to say to those students who were absent from evening prayers: "Remember that the time when you least feel like going to chapel is the time when you most need to go!" He was a fine Christian and a psychologist too.[48]

---

[48] First Published in *Church and Community*, August 1992

The Church needs you

When I was in South India I lived for a while in a town on the plains but at night one could see far away some twenty miles distant the lights of Palni. Palni is situated on the top of a hill and as it says in the Gospel – *A city that is set on a hill cannot be hid*. I believe that the Church should be like that – everywhere to be seen – unequivocal in its beliefs and constant in its service to others. However, the image of the city set on a hill is very properly a reminder of the universal significance of the church; the message of the Good News which the church communicates is a message for all to hear and for all to see and to understand. There is, therefore, an inevitability about the missionary expansion of the church which must be matched with a clear commitment to communicate its message in language and categories of thought which are meaningful to twentieth century man.

Modern Sprotbrough man (have you met him?) has many difficulties with the language used in church. He does not like the language of myths. He finds it difficult to assent to the affirmations about heaven and hell in the creeds. He rightly objects to the language of absolutes, and recognizes that the historical basis of some of the gospel narratives is uncertain. Preaching in the church and Christians in conversation with others must recognize these genuine difficulties as part of the context in which the message of the Good News is to be communicated.

There is another image in the Bible that I like. *The Kingdom of God is like a lamp. Is a lamp brought in to be put under a bushel, or under a bed and not on a stand? For there is nothing hid except to be made manifest, nor is anything secret, except to come to light.* Religious experience is both intellectual and emotional. The lamp shines into the darkness and brings to light our hidden treacheries; it searches the hidden recesses of our personalities and brings into the open our unarticulated fears and our dimly-realized motives. The lamp has also another function; it shows us the way and lights up the way ahead.

One late evening in India I baptized a newly born infant a few hours before he died. The only light in the little hut came from a hurricane lamp and in the heightened shadows one glimpsed the sadness of the parents and shared their feelings of sorrow and disappointment. Yet there was light at the baptism; there was the certainty of God's presence and the love of Christ and his church. The way ahead is a way of joy and sorrow, of happiness and sadness but the light which is Christ shows us the way.

I am reminded of another vivid experience in South India that was when I was waiting in a village to begin a service of worship. I had watched the glorious red and gold of the Indian sunset and suddenly as I waited for the people to come, all was darkness. Then after a few minutes I heard voices in the distance as the people began to assemble for the service. Across the fields I saw one flickering light and then another – and another. The people came one by one or in small groups each carrying a small hurricane light, small snakes of flickering

41

light slowly coming towards me. At last the congregation was assembled; each lamp was placed against another on the floor – and suddenly the whole church was ablaze with light.

If you haven't been to church recently would you regard this letter as an invitation? You will find a warm welcome at any of our church services. It is certainly the case that the church needs you.[49]

---

[49] First Published in **Church and Community**, March 1983

Church Notice Boards

What can we find out about the Sprotbrough Church by looking at its notice boards? Presumably the function of a notice board is first to catch people's attention, and then to give information. For several weeks recently St. Mary's notice board carried the message in bold letters – YOU ARE WELCOME TO OUR SERVICES! Indeed, rumour has it that this particular notice board is so effective that it could be a danger to traffic, or even offend moral sensibilities. Thankfully, so far, St Mary's notice board has carried no message likely to offend, although one could think of a few which might, as for example – Be sure your sins will find you out, or Not many give much to the church nowadays, or even Repent and believe! The trouble with these is that they get a bit too close to the bone to be comfortable. Provided the message does not offend, however, it will be tolerated by most.

The Methodist Church, down the road, does not command such an eye-catching location. Its notice board is a much more low-key affair; its purpose is clearly to provide information rather than to startle thought or evoke interest. It gives useful information, as for example, the name of the church, the name of its minister, the address of the minister's manse and the times of the Sunday services.

So to answer the question with which I started these ruminations, we clearly do not learn very much about the nature of the Church in Sprotbrough from its notice boards. If we would find out more we must enter its doors and venture inside. Inside both churches we would meet ordinary, friendly people like ourselves. We would experience a warm welcome, no doubt, and if we attended to the things that were said, we would find on many occasions much to think and ponder about. Most important of all, we would meet in both congregations people of all kinds of personality, age and temperament, people with doubts and with faith, but all united in a common task of trying to live out their lives according to the principles and pattern of a man who lived long ago and whom today is worshipped as the living God. It's strange but it's true! I know, because I've been inside. I'm reminded of these words of Browning[50]:

> *The very God! think, Abib; dost thou think?*
> *So, the All-Great, were the All-Loving too –*
> *So, through the thunder comes a human voice*
> *Saying, "O heart I made, a heart beats here!*
> *Face my hands fashioned, see it in myself.*
> *Thou hast no power nor may'st conceive of mine.*
> *But love I gave thee, with Myself to love,*
> *And thou must love me who have died for thee!"*
> *The madman saith He said so: it is strange.[51]*

---

[50] Browning, Robert: **Men and Women**, *An Epistle Containing the Strange Medical Experience of Karshish, the Arab Physician,* Lines 304 -11, J M Dent, 1939
[51] First Published in ***Church and Community***, June 1990

Mission

A few weeks ago I preached the sermon in the Methodist Church at a special service which was celebrating "mission". The focus of my sermon was on the Church of South India which was created fifty years ago by the union of Presbyterians, Congregationalists, Methodists and Anglicans. All these parent churches had sent missionaries to South India and the new united church owed a big debt to its parent churches in this country. Now fifty years later, the Church of South India is a strong, independent church from which we in this country have much to learn, not least in how to join together and to live together in unity.

Somewhere near here there is a supermarket with a big sign which reads *We're on a Mission*. The College where I work also has what is called a *Mission Statement*. In both examples the intention is to focus on the main purpose of the organisation, and in both the aim is the same – to offer service to the community. In the case of the supermarket, the mission is to serve the public so that it provides quality groceries at competitive prices; in the case of the college, its mission is to offer quality education and training to all people in Doncaster who can benefit from it. Another example is a business organisation in Barnsley: it describes its mission as to *delight* its customers.

It's good, isn't it, that our modern society has picked up a word from the religious dictionary and applied it to a secular context? Mission is indeed about giving the best we can offer to others in service. It's about looking away from ourselves and concentrating on how best we can *delight* and *serve* our neighbours. The mission of the Church, however, has yet two further dimensions: for Christians, mission involves both obedience and accountability.

So what is our mission? First, we must shun the temptation to become pietistic. Second, our church worship must not be inward looking – that is, being concerned primarily about what goes on inside church buildings. It means accepting the challenge to work within the structures of our divided and fragmented society. Today there is increasingly a division between the rich and the poor – the haves, and the have nots, and globally between the western world and the third world. All around us, near at hand, are people whom we should regard as neighbours – not just because they happen to live in our street, but because Christianity is about caring for others whatever their creed or colour, and irrespective of whether we find them likeable or not! In a wider, global perspective the Christian also regards foreigners in distant lands as his neighbours!

Our mission is to find God in the places of need. That place will often be uncomfortable; it may be disagreeable; and it may be what we least expect to find. But it will be the place of the Cross of Christ.

Mission

We celebrated a mission anniversary: what was that about, I wonder? When I worked in South India I lived in a town called Dharapuram. Twenty miles away I could see the town of Palni and its *Temple* located at the top of a mountain.[52] In India, amongst the Hindus, (as in the Bible), mountains are holy places. At night far away we could see the twinkling lights of the town. It so clearly illustrated the words of Jesus: *"a city that is set on a hill, cannot be hid....."*

The Indian people with whom the early missionaries worked were described in Indian society as *outcastes*. Being an outcaste in India in those days meant regular humiliation and exploitation. No wonder that so many thousands responded to the missionary call of a God who loves everyone whatever their status in society! *Blessed are ye, when men shall revile you, and persecute you, and shall say all manner of evil against you falsely, for my sake...* (Matt 7, v 11) How true this is of the experience of the people in South India, the outcastes, the untouchables, and now often referred to as the Dalits[53].

Blessed! is a particular form of biblical language: it belongs to a type of literature called eschatological – pointing to the end of time. This type of language looks forward to the future blessed state. In this future

---

[52] See also: Letter *The Church Needs You*
[53] The National Campaign on Dalit Human Rights (NCDHR) is part of a wider struggle to abolish "untouchability" and to "cast out caste". "Untouchability" and caste discrimination continue to be a brutal reality for more than 160 million Dalits living in India today, despite the fact that more than half a century has passed since India was born as a "democratic" and independent state. See the Web Site **http://www.dalits.org/**

state the values of the world will be reversed for it will be the establishment of the values of God.

Bonhoeffer comments on the beatitudes with reference to a theology of the cross: "Either I determine the place in which I find God, or I allow God to determine the place where he will be found. If it is I who say where God will be, I will always find there a God who in some way corresponds to me, is agreeable to me, and fits in with my nature. But if it is God who says where He will be, then that truly will be a place which *at first* is not agreeable to me at all, which does not fit so well with me. That place is the cross of Christ. Whoever wishes to find God there, must draw near to the cross in the manner which the Sermon on the Mount requires. This does not correspond with our nature at all".[54]

Our *horizons of expectation* need to be open to change and transformation. The "eternal there and then" becomes our "here and now", not as a faceless principle, but the one who is addressed as *"Maranatha"*. *"Our Lord Cometh"* (1 Cor 16, 22). When he comes, he changes radically our understanding of ourselves, our values and our aspirations.[55]

---

[54] Dietrich Bonhoeffer: Letter to Rüdiger Schleicher, 1936. See also – Dietrich Bonhoeffer: **The Cost of Discipleship**, Peter Smith, 1983
[55] First Published in **Church and Community**, November 1997

Charismatic Christians

The other morning I had the unexpected luxury of being in town with an hour to spare and nothing to do. The car was in the garage and I was absolutely free to do what I liked.   I shall leave readers to anticipate what they would have done in such circumstances; for myself, I bought a copy of *The Times*[56] and read it in the lounge of the *Danum Hotel*.[57]

It was Wednesday July 10th and contained some interesting reading, for example, the defence white paper[58], the re-admission of South Africa to world sport, and a report of the Archbishop of Canterbury's address to an International conference of 2,500 charismatic Christian people in Brighton. What particularly excited my attention was a leading article which deprecated Dr Carey's involvement with the charismatic movement on the grounds that "he might make the church look slightly dotty", or that "he would flirt with religious fanaticism".

---

[56] **The Times**, July 10th 1991
[57] *The Danum Hotel* is situated in Doncaster Town Centre
[58] In July 1991 the **Options for Change** white paper was published. This was the first attempt to redefine the role of the army after the Cold War. It was mainly based on the re-evaluation of Britain's commitment to the defence of West Germany and the restructuring of NATO.

Risking a broad general definition, the charismatic movement is a contemporary movement which has affected a wide spectrum of churches in many countries and it is characterised by a joyful, extrovert approach to worship, often accompanied by chorus singing, the swaying of the body, and the raising of arms. The theological basis of the movement is found in the writing of St Paul and his list of the "gifts of the Spirit" particularly, healings, prophecies and speaking in tongues.

The point of *The Times* leader is that there is a deep incompatibility between the charismatics' beliefs and the character of the Church of England as a broad church. For "with their conviction that they and only they possess the whole truth of Christianity, they are a divisive presence in any denomination". There may be some evidence for this view, but it is also the case, that there are many people who participate in charismatic worship services who do not display intolerance of others' views and who are not divisive influences in a congregation.

There are three issues regarding this matter, however, which deserve further exploration: the first is to look sympathetically but critically at the phenomenon of tongue-speaking; the second is to consider what we mean when we address God as Holy Spirit, and third is to see what we can learn from the movement about enriching our Sunday worship. Glossalalia (tongue speaking) is best understood within the psychology of religious behaviour as a form of prayer, for as far as I am aware, examples which have been studied have not exhibited any of the salient features of a language.[59]

The doctrine of God the Holy Spirit embraces all the ways in which God encounters the human spirit, both within the church and without it; we would be unwise to imagine that God's dealings with us are limited to a narrow personal view of religious experience. In the best charismatic worship, there is a sense of peace and joy, and there is space for each individual to be herself; there is no bullying, no high pressure evangelism, no desire to make everyone the same as everyone else.

Instead, there is the opportunity for each person to be open to the possibility of an encounter with God. And in the end, of course, what matters is not our feeble, fumbling attempts to worship God, but what God does to us when he comes to us, and like Mary in the garden, and Thomas in the upper room, calls us by our name, It's interesting isn't it – when one has an hour to spare?[60]

---

[59] See Samarin W. J: **Tongues of Men and Angels: the Religious Language of Pentecostalism**, Collier Macmillan, 1972

[60] First Published in ***Church and Community***, September 1991

Stories

Here are three stories. The first is about clamping.[61] The second is about an anti-racist march that went wrong. The third is about pit closures.

The other day I observed an enterprising young man removing the front wheel of his car plus the clamp that had been firmly placed around it. His intention was clearly not to pay the fine and to drive off with the clamp in his boot! But should he have been clamped in the first place? One has sympathy with the victim but also perhaps with the person who placed the clamp on the car!

Last Saturday, a huge anti-racist march took place in Welling, in Kent.[62] The intention was to provide a powerful visible protest against the explicit racism of the National Front Party. You will have read the reports, no doubt, of the confrontation that ensued between a small

---

[61] *Note:* This is a system introduced in the UK in the 1990s to deter motorists from parking illegally at roadsides or in private spaces.
[62] An anti-racist demonstration of 50,000 marched through the streets of Welling on **October 16th 1993** in a determined attempt to shut down the headquarters of the extremist British Nationalist Party. Reports suggested over-reaction by the police who would not allow demonstrators to walk past the BNP HQ. Subsequently eight people were jailed on **13th September 1995** for taking part in the demonstration and attacking the police.

number of trouble-makers and the police. However, many innocent people got caught up in the violence and over sixty people were injured. You might have seen pictures on television of the mayhem, red smoke bombs, and mounted police in riot gear. If you are a *Guardian* reader, you will have read in the correspondence, claim and counter-claim, and assertions of the basic right to protest peacefully, and of what counts as responsible and irresponsible police action.

Nearer to home, and all around us are mining communities threatened by the latest news of pit closures.[63] For some it will mean the opportunity to train successfully for a new career; but for many the reality will be the indignity of unemployment and a huge loss of income. Most certainly, what were once lively, thriving communities will go into inevitable decline with untold human suffering in consequence. Whilst Britain loses its mines, however, one learns that market forces impose the need to import cheaper coal from overseas.[64]

There are at least three things to say about each of these true stories: each describes a facet of our modern society, each poses a moral dilemma, and to each there is no straightforward answer. But all the stories raise questions of conflicting values which need to be examined. Someone once said: "Stories tell us about ourselves – How true that is![65]

---

[63] See House of Commons Hansard Debates for 17 Mar 1993
[64] A powerful film **Brassed Off** was screened in 1996 depicting the devastating effects of the closure of the pit on a South Yorkshire mining community
[65] First Published in **Church and Community**, November 1993

Kafka's Parable

Some of the best known stories in the Bible are the parables of Jesus. I expect that most people remember the stories of the Good Samaritan, the Prodigal Son and the Labourers in the Vineyard. I wonder how many you recall, of the other thirty-seven parables that Jesus told?

Parable is a particular form of literature; its purpose is to subvert our normal understanding. Its aim is to jolt us into a different way of looking at things. Hence, the despised Samaritan would be the very last person a Jew would imagine in the role of rescuer. Throwing a party to celebrate the return of the son who has wasted all his father's money was from the elder son's point of view both inappropriate and unfair. To distribute wages according to the length of time worked in the vineyard was reasonable and just, but why give everyone exactly the same? That surely cannot be right, or can it?

Here is a modern parable from Kafka, the twentieth century Austrian novelist.[66] A man wants to see The Law but a doorkeeper who tells him to wait bars his admission. The man waits and waits and from time to time remonstrates with the doorkeeper. He is advised that it is no use trying to push past the doorkeeper because inside there are further doors with bigger and stronger doorkeepers who will not let

---

[66] Franz Kafka **The Trial**, Minerva Paperback Edition, 1994

him pass. Finally, when the man is dying he makes one last plea. The doorkeeper replies: "For every person there is one door and this particular door is intended for you. Only you could gain admittance through this door but I am now going to shut it".

What is the meaning of Kafka's parable? What new insight does it provide for us? It raises the question doesn't it, of whether life is like a door intended for each one of us alone but through which we can never pass? To understand and accept this possibility enables us to come to terms with unrealised hopes, unfulfilled dreams, with disappointments and despairs. Yet what <u>doors</u> are we still knocking at which can never be opened to us? What other <u>doors</u> should we be seeking to open?

The purpose of this parable is to subvert, to jolt, to surprise, to undermine our normal expectation of the way things are, and thereby to allow the possibility of a new perspective. Jesus taught in parables to jerk people into a different perception of what is possible. The irony is this: Jesus, the supreme teller of parables himself became a parable. The cross of Jesus especially subverts our normal expectation of things. The powerless becomes powerful. Ignorance becomes wisdom. The weak becomes strong. The fearful becomes fearless. Pain and suffering is transformed into victory.

> "Everyone shall be remembered,
> but each became great in proportion to his expectation.
> One became great by expecting the possible, another by expecting the eternal,

but he who expected the impossible became greater than all.
Everyone shall be remembered,
but each was great in proportion, to the greatness of that with which he
strove." [67] [68]

---

[67] Soren Kierkegaard, **Fear and Trembling,** Penguin August 1985
[68] First Published in *Church and Community*, August 1995

Reading the Bible

It's mid August. The family is going away on holiday and a variety of reading tastes is hidden amongst the clothes in the suitcase. I notice a medley of titles: *Hammer of Mars, Star Trek, Red Dwarf, Europe Unfolding, Virgil's Aeneid, The Moonstone, Blood Sisters,* and *Don't Laugh at Fools.* I push in between the socks a couple of theological books and a copy of the latest *Jeffrey Archer.*

Why do people choose books anyway? Our choice of titles is unlikely to be random. We often choose books of authors we already know and like, and about subjects we are already interested in. Psychologists might tell us that our selection of books is self-revelatory, that is, it provides insight into the kind of people we are. I wonder what our choice reveals about us! I suppose the same applies to newspapers and magazines; why do people still read *The Guardian* when they can now purchase *The Times* and *The Independent* at a much cheaper price? And why read *The Guardian* anyway, why not *The Mirror,* or *The Sun?*

Another intriguing question is what presuppositions we bring to the things we read. For whenever we pick up a book or a newspaper we already have knowledge, experience, prejudices and insights which affect our understanding of the text we read. If we wish to allow the book, the report or the story to influence our thinking we need to be aware of these prior meanings which can directly affect our

understanding.   Please test the validity of what I have just written.
How often have you started to read something and thrown it down
before you have finished it!   Why did you stop reading it...?

Most important of all, how do we read and interpret the Bible? The
Bible has a special and central place in our faith and worship.   It
informs our doctrines, inspires our worship, and influences our
behaviour. However, as with the reading of any other literature we
need to discard our presuppositions and prejudices first before the
biblical text can address us, and speak to our condition.
Understanding the Bible is about *the fusion of horizons*. *Our horizon* is the
limited circle of our vision, of our thought, as determined by the place
where we stand.   When we allow the Bible to speak to us, *our horizon* is
re-oriented, re-constructed, transformed by *the horizon of the text*.

Let me suggest a few examples. Is the saga of Moses a story which
describes liberation from slavery, or is it a commemoration of victory
by the strong over the weak?   Both interpretations are possible
although one is more popular than the other.   Is the parable of the
workers in the vineyard a blueprint for labour relations, or is it a
celebration of the grace and love of God for sinners?   Was the reply
of Jesus to the question about giving taxes to Caesar a definitive ruling
about obedience to the state, or was it a clever but ambiguous answer
given in a situation where he had been put in a tight corner by his
opponents?   Is the central point of the Christmas story about the
birth of a poor child who became a refugee and was persecuted by the
rulers of the land he was in, or is it about harmony, peace and

goodwill? Both interpretations are offered at Christmas although one usually receives more emphasis than the other.

Finally, if we are able to recognise our *prior understandings* and discard them for a moment in order to allow the text to speak to our condition what is our response to those beatitudes in Matthew's gospel – *Blessed are the meek, the merciful, the peacemakers and the persecuted?* What also is our response to the recorded words of Jesus on the cross: *Father forgive them, for they know not what they do?*[69]

---

[69] First Published in **Church and Community**, September 1994

Safe In The Last Homely House

Frodo was now safe in the Last Homely House east of the Sea. That house was, as Bilbo had long ago reported, 'a perfect house, whether you like food or sleep, or story-telling or singing, or just sitting and thinking best, or a pleasant mixture of them all.' Merely to be there was a cure for weariness, fear, and sadness.[70]

Frodo, the Hobbit, was the bearer of the magic ring and had just narrowly escaped death. Now after a long period of recuperation he was feeling well again, and safe. All of us can identify with his feelings: there are so many things that we would like to enjoy but cannot because of our particular circumstances. How wonderful it would be wouldn't it, to be in a perfect house, and to have a cure for weariness, fear and sadness?

I know well that some of us have hearts so heavy with grief that we wonder whether the sadness will ever leave us. Some of us have an incurable illness. Some of us have fears, so deep in our sub-conscious that we find them hard to articulate. Some of us live with a daily experience of physical pain. Some of us have a nagging sense of guilt that we try to dispel but which keeps resurfacing. Some of us have broken relationships that we long to heal. Wouldn't it be splendid if all this sadness could be dispelled and if we could suddenly find ourselves in the *Last Homely House east of the Sea?*

---

[70] J R R Tolkien: **The Lord of the Rings**, Harper Collins, 1991, page 241

Safe In The Last Homely House

Tolkien's picture of the *Last Homely House* reminds me of the vivid description of the *New Jerusalem* found in the last chapter of the Bible. It describes a city that does not need the sun or the moon because *the glory of God gives it light* and its gates are never shut. It is a place of pure delight where *there will be no more death or mourning or crying or pain.* This loving description of heaven was written at a time of great persecution and suffering to give comfort and hope. It was a message for those who anticipated certain death to assure them of the total presence of God in all human experience. As St Paul wrote in his Letter to the Romans: *If we live, we live to the Lord; and if we die, we die to the Lord. So, whether we live or die, we belong to the Lord.* The truth is that God is always with us in every experience that we undergo.

But there is a difference between Tolkien and Revelation. Tolkien, although clearly influenced by biblical imagery, is describing hopes, dreams and the reality of the present. Frodo the Hobbit is very much alive. He is weak from his illness, tired from his journey and chastened by his suffering – but he is safe! Moreover he is stronger and more confident as a result of his experiences.

Christianity does not provide an escape from human vicissitudes. On the contrary! The Church is meant to be a place where we can feel safe – safe to be ourselves, safe in the company of others, and most important of all – safe in the knowledge of a loving God, who experiences our suffering with us, and who travels with us all the way.[71]

---

[71] First Published in **Church and Community**, August 2004

St Mary's Parish Church

Sprotbrough
Methodist Church

Christians and Politics

Christianity and Politics

We have watched with hope and admiration the recent student movement for democracy in China, and then with dismay and horror the ruthless way it was crushed.[72] Even as I write, news is reaching us of more arrests and of tighter army control. In the last few years, educational, cultural and church contacts between China and the west have signalled the possibility of closer communication and understanding. We hope that present events will not reverse these developments. We must urge our political leaders to condemn the atrocities whilst keeping open the lines of communication: a delicate and prudent task?

The Salman Rushdie affair has shocked us too. Many Muslims themselves share our abhorrence at the outrageous call to kill Mr Rushdie. However ill judged the content of the book, *The Satanic Verses*,[73] Christians can understand the Muslim belief that the Qur'an, which is their sacred book, has been insulted. For Muslims the Qur'an is the evidence of the divine manifestation to believers. To dishonour the Qur'an is to dishonour God. We can understand, therefore, Muslims' feelings and can recognise why they feel angry and hurt. We have been amazed in recent days to see millions of people in Iran

---

[72] On June 3 and 4, 1989, the Communist People's Liberation Army in China brutally crushed supporters of democracy who marched on Tiananmen Square in Beijing. Hundreds of students and others were killed.

[73] Salman Rushdie: **The Satanic Verses**, Viking Press, February 1989

united in a fanaticism of grief for the late Ayatollah Khomeni. We wonder what consequences will flow from the change of leadership there and whether it will lead to a lessening of international tension. We can certainly make a start here in Sprotbrough. Do we know any Muslim people? We can at least enter into conversation with them.

As I write this, it is a beautiful summer day. How pleasant it might be if we could forget the political realities of the world and just bask in our insularity! That is not the way of being a Christian. To follow Christ means to follow him into the entire world – to preach the good news of the gospel most certainly, but within the realities of the social, cultural and political contexts of our times. That means, then, giving support to those agencies which work in other parts of the world, for example, missionary societies, the United Nations Organisation, Christian Aid and Save the Children. It also means scrutinising with care the foreign policies of our government and those of the opposition parties. "A good Christian", someone once said, "holds her Bible in one hand, and her newspaper in the other, and reads each in relation to the other."[74]

---

[74] First Published in *Church and Community*, July 1989

General Election 1983

As I write this, the date of the general election has been announced and all of us, as responsible citizens should vote on June 9th. What will be the factors which will influence the electorate's decision of whom to vote for, I wonder? Some will vote for the party of which they are members; others for the party which they have always supported in the past. I would like to think that many people (perhaps the majority if the opinion polls are to be believed) at present undecided, will examine the issues, read the manifestos of the various parties, weigh carefully the alternatives which are proposed and will vote accordingly.

As Christians, I believe, we belong to that majority – that is, we must examine the issues before we vote. I believe that we have this obligation because we live in a complex society and because there are few easy quick solutions to the problems that we face. Simple answers are likely to be simplistic. For example, we abhor violence and we hate war; but we are members of a secular society and we pay the taxes, like everybody else, which support our armed forces and which continue the arms race. We cannot appeal to the Bible as the grounds for our moral choices either, because (a) there are moral objections to making God the ground of our moral judgements, and (b) anyway, how can we be sure that we know God's will in any particular moral case? Therefore, we need to examine most carefully what the parties promise about the issues that concern us all, both with regard to the quality of life in our society and with reference to international questions of peace and war, wealth and poverty, trade and immigration.

How can the responsible Christian citizen disentangle this complexity? The distinguishing mark of a Christian is love and it is this dynamic which must surely influence the way we vote on June 9th. Christian love follows the pattern of one who identified himself with the underprivileged, the outcast, the diseased, the rejected, the dispossessed, the lonely and the hungry. Christianity is not a separate, isolated, feeble, apolitical religion; it is the religion of those who follow Christ into the suffering world to redeem it.

Someone once said that man's theological affirmations are always statements about his self-understanding, that is, if you want to discover what man is – look at what he says about God. Perhaps we could say, if you want to discover what a Christian is – look at the way he votes![75]
[76]

---

[75] The actual result on June 9th 1983 was 397 Conservatives; 209 Labour; 23 Liberal/SDP Alliance; 21 others = 650 MPs in total. Margaret Thatcher's second election victory in 1983 was one of the most decisive in post-war Britain. The Conservatives benefited from a three horse race, in which votes for the opposition were split between the Labour Party and the Liberal/SDP Alliance. Mrs Thatcher saw her majority rise to 144 seats. In terms of share of the vote, Labour only just managed to come in ahead of the Alliance, in their worst election performance since 1918.
(Source: http://www.bbc.co.uk/politics97)
[76] First Published in *Church and Community*, June 1983

General Election 1987

Two anxieties often beset the Christian. One is the fear of being out of touch with the demands of today's world, of being thought irrelevant. The other concern is that by becoming involved in the political affairs of the world one might forget the essential task of witnessing to and proclaiming the gospel. The problem is real but the theological answer at least is simple: the gospel has to be proclaimed and understood within the political and social structures of our time. In fighting racism, sexism, oppression, injustice and untruths of every kind, we discover the context in which the gospel is to be announced.

In the General Election each of us has an opportunity to bring together our religious and political commitments; first in our reflection on how we ought to vote, and second, in actually placing our vote in the ballot box. When reading a report of the recent local elections I was very sorry to see that in our local constituency, Southern Parks, only just over 40% of eligible voters had actually voted. I was sorry even though compared with other wards, in terms of the level of participation, this was one of the better results. If you were one of those who did not vote on May 7th, may I ask you to make sure you vote on June 11th? [77]

---

[77] The Election Result on June 11th 1987 returned 650 MPs to Parliament: 376 Conservatives; 229 Labour; 22 Lib/SDP Alliance; 23 Others.

How should a Christian vote? I am sure that of we all know good, honourable Christian people who are sincere Socialists, or committed Conservatives, or active Alliance supporters. According to the *Sunday Times*, most of the national daily newspapers have already come out strongly in favour of the Tories. No doubt this will be a strong influence on some people. But am I naive in thinking this is a pity? Before the election has begun many have already made up their minds. I hope that we shall not be swayed by reports of opinion polls. Already, it seems to me, newspapers are giving more prominence to reporting the results of opinion polls, than to providing balanced debate of the critical issues.

Here in Sprotbrough, where do we stand? I hope that we shall reflect on the issues, read carefully the manifestos, listen critically to the speeches, and test the claims of our political leaders against principles derived from the reading of the Christian gospel, in terms of a vision of God's kingdom. There are many who will try to influence us; let us at least keep our integrity and be our own man. Here are some of the questions which we need to examine before we place our vote: unemployment, defence and nuclear weapons; assistance to the third world; education. What practical solutions do our politicians offer? How realistic are they? How do they compare with the values that we most cherish for our society and for our children?

The following two quotations are relevant here. Vote as you think, not as others tell you to vote!

"It takes courage to experience the freedom that comes with autonomy, courage to accept intimacy and directly encounter other persons, courage to take a stand in an unpopular cause, courage to choose authenticity over approval, and to choose it again and again, courage to accept the responsibility for your own choices and indeed, courage to be the very unique person you really are". [78]

"To be nobody but yourself in a world which is doing its best, night and day to make you everybody else – means to fight the hardest battle which any human being can fight; and never stop fighting". [79] [80]

---

[78] James M & Jongeward D: **Born to Win**, Signet 1978
[79] Cummings E.E: **A Miscellany**, Harcourt Brace Jovanovich, Inc. 1955
[80] First Published in ***Church and Community***, June 1987

General Election 1992

As a young teenager in my local church in Nottingham I was made Christian Citizenship Secretary. In those days I tended to see social issues as black or white, as entirely good or totally evil. Either one was a pacifist totally and utterly, or one was a war mongerer! Either one was in favour of teetotalism or one was a drunkard! Looking back to that formative period of my life I blush at my youthful intolerance and at my failure to recognise that moral choice is seldom a clear-cut affair.

Moral choice must arise from a view of several perspectives; points for and against have to be considered. Moral action, therefore, is a question of balancing points in favour with points against and then putting one's decision into practice. That, of course, is exactly what each of us is required to do on April 9th.[81] Voting in a general election is moral action, based on principles that have been carefully thought through and evaluated. So let me suggest a few principles that should guide us as we take our part in choosing a new government:

(1) We are faced by opposing ideologies – capitalism, socialism and liberal democracy. Although there is much in common between the stances and programmes of the three main parties, there are also clear differences of policy and principle amongst them. Much of the

---

[81] The Election Result on April 9th 1992 returned 651 MPs to Parliament: 336 Conservatives; 271 Labour; 22 Liberal Democrat; 24 Others

difference hangs on the concept of a just society and on the issue of (a) how wealth is to be created, and (b) how it is to be distributed.

(2) We are confronted by political image-makers and propagandists. All the psychological methods available are ranged against us in attempts to influence our voting behaviour. We should be alert to these persuasive techniques and not allow ourselves to be unduly influenced by them. For example, we should look at the content of what is said, and not at the level of the attractiveness of the communicator. We should weigh the arguments presented to us with care, and should look for balanced factual statement rather than emotive rhetoric.

(3) As Christian citizens we stand for truth, justice, and peace in our society (others stand for these things too) and indeed for all people whatever their creed or nationality. Our vote, therefore, should be cast not for the party that offers most personal gain, but for the party that looks most likely to promote the welfare of all its citizens. It was the prophet Amos who said: *"Let justice roll down like waters, and righteousness like an ever flowing stream"*. It was Jesus who interpreted the parable of the Good Samaritan with the injunction "go and do likewise", and who said that those who will inherit the Kingdom are those who feed the hungry, give drink to the thirsty, care for the sick, and visit the prisoners.

I hope, therefore, that we shall cast our votes on April 9th not out of dull habit, but because we have pondered the principles, evaluated the manifestos, and made our choice accordingly.[82]

---

[82] First Published in *Church and Community*, April 1992

Racism, Capitalism and Religious Belief

I was talking to a Salesman on the telephone.

'What is your name?' I enquired.

'Mr Zi.'

'Mr Zi? That sounds like a foreign name.'

'It depends which country you're in, Sir.'

I accepted the rebuke. But of course, Mr Zi was right. In so many ways our interpretation of events depends on what side we are on, or in Mr Zi's words, what country we inhabit.   Let me develop this thought with reference to three examples.

First, racism. The recent reports of the ongoing Stephen Lawrence Enquiry[83] in London have shown that being a black person is a distinct disadvantage if you live in London, and particularly if you have dealings with the Police.   One might go further and accuse the Metropolitan Police of being riddled with racist attitudes and procedures.   But *Sir Paul Condon*, the Metropolitan Chief Commissioner, has denied that this is the case.   It all depends of course on which side you are on, or as Mr Zi would say, which country you're in.

---

[83] The Home Secretary on 31st July 1997 announced a Judicial Inquiry into the death of Stephen Lawrence who was murdered by racists on 22 April 1993. The Report of Sir William MacPherson was subsequently published on Wednesday 24th February 1999.

A second example is capitalism. *The Times* today[84] reports the fear of a meltdown in world stock markets and a decline into 1930s' style economic depression. Recent years have seen an expansion in the wealth of western economies matched by an increasing mountain of debt in the Third World. Gordon Brown, the Chancellor of the Exchequer, has taken a leading role in the meetings this weekend of the Group of Seven Industrial Nations to press for greater debt relief for the world's poorest countries. It is pleasing to note that the final communiqué of the G7 meetings was to sustain the momentum of HIPC.[85] Therefore, as we view with alarm the fall in the values of stocks and shares, perhaps we should consider sympathetically the situation of those countries in the developing world where the present global economic crisis is hitting hardest.

A third example is religious belief. It is reported today[86] that the famous social psychologist, Professor Michael Argyle, has spent fifteen years studying what makes us happy. He has concluded that millions of soap fans are some of the happiest. Other sources of happiness are sports and leisure activities, marriage (especially for men), and church-going. According to his research regular church-goers were much happier than non-believers. Well, I suppose none of these findings is surprising, but it does make us think. He suggests that watching Coronation Street, playing cricket, having a good wife, and going to Church, fulfil a common need – they make us happy. One activity is as good as another. Well, what do you think? Is that why we go to

---

[84] **The Times**, October 5th, 1998
[85] HIPC = Heavily Indebted Poor Country
[86] **The Guardian**, October 5th, 1998

Church?   Is that all?   It depends, as Mr Zi would say, which country you are in.[87]

---

[87] First Published in *Church and Community*, November 1998

The Dam Busters

I wonder how often in a day or even in a week we find time to think about God? Unless we are particularly religious and say our prayers every day, or make a special point of going to church regularly, I dare say that most of us, to be honest, do not spend much time thinking about God at all.

Nearly fifty years ago, the German pastor Bonhoeffer described such a position as a sign of having grown up. The mature modern Christian has learnt, he said, to live without the God hypothesis. In other words, "man come of age"[88] has learnt to accept personal responsibility for the way he lives life without needing to bring God into the discussion at all. Bonhoeffer, of course, was not abandoning Christian faith, far from it, and he knew more than most what the cost of discipleship really was. Right to the end of his life when he was executed by the Germans, he remained a deeply devout Christian believer.

The scars of that war, of the bombing, and the killing remain with us fifty years later. We have learnt indeed to live without *the God hypothesis*. Much more disturbingly, many have learnt, it would seem, to live without God at all. As one writer has recently put it: "The divine presence has been a palpable absence in our culture since Auschwitz

---

[88] that is, man who has come of age, grown up, matured etc.

so that generations have grown up and now live without any awareness even of that absence".[89]

These words need deeply pondering. They describe so well the irony, even the sadness of our modern predicament. Modern man has grown up so that he is ignorant even of the possibility of the reality of God. It's like an orphan growing up, not just missing his father, but not even being able to understand what it would be like to have a father. It's akin to someone who is so profoundly deaf that not only is he unable to appreciate the exhilaration and delight of music, but he cannot even imagine what the experience of listening to music would be like. It's as though being blind, so terribly blind, that one cannot conceive or imagine the beauty of a smile in a lover's eyes, or the serenity of a landscape, or the texture and form of a painting.

This month the RAF is commemorating the Dam Busters' Raid,[90] and a special programme of *Songs of Praise*[91] has been televised combining Red Arrows[92] and prayers for reconciliation. That event from fifty

---

[89] Carroll I R P, *Review of George Steiner's Real Presences: Is there anything in what we say?* Faber and Faber, 1989, **Scottish Journal of Theology,** Vol 46, No 1, 1993, page 103.

[90] 16 May 1993 was the 50th anniversary of the famous **Dam Busters** raid by No 617 Squadron led by Wing Commander Guy Gibson who was awarded the Victoria Cross for his part in it. Nineteen *Avro Lancaster* bombers attacked the Möhne, Eder and Sorpe dams in Germany, armed with the famous *bouncing bomb.* 476 Germans and 593 Ukrainian and Dutch labourers, and French and Belgian Prisoners of War were reported killed as a consequence of the raid.

[91] **Songs of Praise** is a popular programme of hymn singing televised by the BBC on Sunday evenings

[92] *The Red Arrows* is the well known aerobatic team described as *the public face of the Royal Air Force.* The Red Arrows exists to demonstrate the professional

years ago reminds us both of the evil of war and of the heroism and self-sacrifice of which man is capable. In a strange way, it reminds us both of the *absence* and of the *presence* of God. In the midst of war there is talk of forgiveness. In war-torn contemporary Europe, in famine stricken Africa, in our village community and in our personal relationships there is a need for us at least to be aware of the absence. . … And beyond that?

There is a clear requirement for the life of the churches to become places where we can engage with one another and with our neighbours in dialogue. Perhaps most of all, our church services should unambiguously celebrate God's presence, characterised by open and genuine opportunities for reflection and encounter, where in an atmosphere of prayer and worship all may honestly be themselves, perhaps just to be quiet, or to think, or to pray.[93]

---

excellence of the RAF and promote recruitment to the RAF. (See **http://www.redarrows.com**)
[93] First Published in ***Church and Community***, June 1993

Destruction of the Twin Towers

September 11th 2001 is a day none of us will ever forget. The terrifying imagery of that day, vividly reported on our television screens and described in appalling detail in our newspapers, ensures that the attacks on the World Trade Centre and the Pentagon are stamped indelibly on our conscience. Combating international terrorism has become a key objective in the foreign policies of western and developing nations alike. A problem, of course, is how international terrorism is to be defined? The heinous crimes of those who perpetrated the September 11th attacks must be considered alongside the bombing of innocent victims in the war in Afghanistan, the vile attacks by suicide bombers on Israeli civilians, and the wicked and ruthless suppression of the Palestinians by Israel.

In deliberately deploying these adjectives I may rightly be accused of emotivism, of over-simplification even, but not of exaggeration. The continuing conflict between India and Pakistan over Kashmir[94], the danger of American unilateral military action against the threat of Iraq[95], and the continuing violence between Israel and Palestine[96] are

---

[94] Early in 2004 relations between India and Pakistan remarkedly improved.

[95] The USA and the UK embarked on a war with Iraq in the Spring of 2003 amidst wide international condemnation. On 28-June-2004 the USA returned sovereignty to Iraq and a new interim government was sworn in. By July 2005 conditions in Iraq were much improved but daily violence and deaths of soldiers and civilians was continuing.

[96] In January 2005 Ariel Sharon, the Israeli leader had welcomed measures taken by the new Palestinian President, Mahmoud Abbas, to fight terror. By July 2005 the

the political realities to which responsible government must respond. It shows a culpable lack of insight, therefore, to depict the present international scene as simply a conflict between good and evil. Rather, it is surely a combination of a number of factors – including the psychology of those who see themselves powerless in the face of power, of those who are hungry and destitute in a world of affluent plenty, and of those who are crushed by an overwhelming sense of injustice. Also it is naive to deplore and condemn the abominable excesses of those driven to terrorism unless one also recognises the inherent clash of values, ideologies and religious fanaticisms that underlie them.

What then can we do in response to these immensely challenging and frightening times? First, we must recognise that "no man is an island..."[97], and that we live in a global community in which the suffering of other human beings, wherever they live, is indeed a matter for our concern.[98] Second, we applaud the increased international aid offered by our government[99] and in addition we respond, as much as we are able, to special appeals from Aid Organisations working in

---

situation was improving. Despite continued violence there was optimism that Israel would fulfil its promise to pull back troops from West Bank cities.

[97] John Donne, **Devotions upon Emergent Occasions**, 1624

[98] Ibid: *No man is an island, entire of itself; every man is a piece of the continent, a part of the main. If a clod be washed away by the sea, Europe is the less, as well as if a promontory were, as well as if a manor of thy friend's or of thine own were: any man's death diminishes me, because I am involved in mankind, and therefore never send to know for whom the bells tolls; it tolls for thee.*

[99] Gordon Brown, the Chancellor of the Exchequer, announced an increase in Overseas Aid in the <u>Comprehensive Spending Review</u> on Monday, 15 July 2002: a rise from the then 0.32% of GNP per year to 0.4% by 2006.

famine-torn areas of the world[100]. Third, we have a liberal, tolerant, compassionate and welcoming attitude towards genuine asylum seekers. Fourth, we rejoice in the reality of a multi-faith society in which people of all religions and none, can live together in communities vividly enriched by the thought, language and cultures of people from a variety of backgrounds. Fifth, (and paradoxically) the Christian interpretation of the *Letter to the Hebrews*[101] suggests that Christian people are on a journey and that in this world we have no permanent home! For we are all strangers and pilgrims! Yet to belong to God's kingdom is to know that ultimately we shall no longer be strangers and foreigners[102] for we are destined to live in a city whose builder and maker is God.[103] That city is the Christian's ultimate destination; it is to find himself totally in the loving presence of Almighty God.

---

[100] See UNICEF web site at http://www.unicef.org.uk/
[101] Hebrews, 13 v 14; 11 v 13; 13 v 2; and 11v 10
[102] Ephesians 2, verse 19 AV
[103] First Published in **Church and Community**, September 2002 and in the **Church and Society Newsletter** of the Sheffield Methodist District and Society Unit Committee Autumn 2002

Deep Impact and Deep Tragedy

On July 4th some astonishing pictures flashed around the world. The NASA discovery mission *Deep Impact* had successfully achieved its first objective. A small copper spacecraft, the size of a washing machine, weighing 820 pounds and equipped with camera and radio, crashed at a speed of 23,000 miles per hour into the *Comet Tempel 1*. The collision created an immense flash of light. Nearby, 300 miles away, the mothership monitored and photographed the explosion. The spacecraft had been launched on January 12th and 172 days later, after a journey of 268 million miles, with accurate prediction it crashed spectacularly into the surface of the comet. *Deep Impact* is the first space mission to probe beneath the surface of a comet and reveal the secrets of its interior.[104]

One admires the mathematical and technological skill of the NASA scientists. Even more remarkable, however, are marvellous developments in the field of cosmology.[105] For example, there is the theory of *panspermia* suggesting the possibility that life existed <u>before</u> the solar system was even formed. There is also the belief that the universe did not start with a big bang as previously thought – but that

---

[104] Comets are time capsules that hold clues about the formation and evolution of the solar system. They are composed of ice, gas and dust – primitive debris from the solar system's distant and coldest regions that formed 4.5 billion years ago.

[105] Cosmology is that branch of physics which studies the structure and evolution of the universe as a whole and is probably the field of science that intersects most directly with theology.

there was first a *huge inflationary burst of energy,* then *the big bang,* then an *expanding universe* ever since. The more I learn about *the fabric of the cosmos*[106] the greater my surprise and delight.

On July 7th, three days after the huge success of the NASA mission, some more photographs flashed around the world – this time they were horrific images of the aftermath of a terrorist attack on London in which over fifty people were killed and countless others maimed and disfigured for life. The Archbishop of Canterbury, commented: *"Dead silence, except for the occasional sirens. That was how people were describing what it was like in London yesterday afternoon. Just as when we face a personal shock or loss, there comes a moment when we don't know what to say, or how we feel, or what can be done: dead silence".*[107] But Rowan Williams also suggested that we must take courage, and reminded his listeners of the words of St Paul: *"We don't know how to pray or what to hope for sometimes. But the spirit of God is working with us, and even our wordless cries and groans become part of the Spirit's action".*

Deep impact and deep tragedy. Each of us will know someone who can echo these words with poignant feeling and understanding. The easy answer to explain human wickedness, evil, suffering and tragic death is somehow to blame God, or at least, to ask what he was doing about it! But the Christian's response is very different. We sit alongside the sufferer. Perhaps we remain silent? Perhaps we utter

---

[106] Brian Greene: **The Fabric of the Cosmos**, Penguin, 2005
[107] The Most Rev. Rowan Williams, **Thought for the Day**, BBC4, 8 July 2005

wordless cries and groans? Perhaps *"we weep with those who weep"*?[108] At the centre of our understanding – is our faith, far more awesome than space technology and cosmological discovery, that deep in the heart of the universe is a God who meets us in a man hanging on a cross. Only that sort of faith enables me to make some sense of the appalling scenes that we have witnessed in London this week.[109]

---

[108] Romans 12, verse 15
[109] First Published in *Church and Community*, August, 2005

Let there be Light

When I was seventeen years old I remember walking through a park in Nottingham late at night and gazing with wonder at the immense and beautiful night sky. Now, fifty years later, in blissful years of retirement, I have started this activity again not in Nottingham but in Cusworth Park, Doncaster. Now, as then, I am filled with a sense of awesome delight as with members of the Doncaster Astronomical Society I look at the spangled heavens above. However, there is an important difference: with the aid of the Society's computerised telescope, I am able now (like Galileo who in 1610 was the first person to turn a telescope to the sky) to examine the hills and cavities of the moon, and the rings around Saturn. I am astonished to view the brilliance of Sirius and to see the beauty of Venus; and millions of light years away I glimpse the clusters of stars in distant galaxies.

As a student of astronomy I am learning to recognise some of the eighty-eight constellations that appear in the night sky, for example, *Andromeda,* a large spiral galaxy 2.3 million light years away, and the magnificent *Orion* with its shape of a hunter brandishing his raised club and shield, and *Ursa Major* (The Great Bear) with its seven main stars often referred to as *The Plough.* When I attend meetings of the Society I am constantly introduced to a new language which speaks of white dwarfs, red dwarfs, neutron stars, black holes and dark matter. Astronomy is an exciting, demanding and fascinating field of study.

Astronomy is a branch of physical science that aims to describe what is the case, that is, to uncover facts about the earth, the planets, the stars and the universe. Strictly speaking astronomy asks the questions what and how. But I wish to ask another question – why? I suppose it is like falling in love! You can explain why the girl is attractive (or the man?), you can describe her appearance and the sound of her voice, but that doesn't explain why. Why, of all the girls you have met, was it this particular girl with whom you fell in love? So with astronomy – we can study the details of the universe, we can feel excited and thrilled at the theories of the scientists about how the universe began – but it still leaves the "why questions" unanswered. Being a religious sort of person, I want to ask what astronomers and physicists cannot tell me, whether God had anything to do with it.[110]

For thousands of years the Church has believed that God created the world out of nothing. This doctrine was called *creation ex nihilo*. It is interesting that today, a common view amongst astronomy scientists, suggests that the universe did indeed begin absolutely "from nothing". For example – Steven Hawking, the famous Cambridge physicist has said that "almost everyone now believes that the universe and time itself had a beginning at the big bang" (Hawking and Penrose, 1996, 20).

---

[110] A highly acclaimed book on the mystery of the Universe is – Brian Greene: **The Fabric of the Cosmos**, Penguin, 2005

So I continue to ask why?   Also how? How can the universe have come into existence from nothing?   The very idea seems absurd! The philosopher William Craig[111] suggests that a possible theological explanation is to think of God as existing timelessly *sans universe*, that is, independently of the universe, and that God becomes temporal at the moment of creation and at the origin of time.   However, some four hundred and fifty years before the birth of Christ a Jewish philosopher said:

> *"In the beginning, God created the heaven and the earth"*

and perhaps even more profoundly:

> *"God said, Let there be light: and there was light."*

Perhaps the conclusion of recent research in astronomical science is coming very close to the ancient doctrine of the church that God created the world out of nothing? Maybe that is a sufficient answer? Or perhaps not? In the meantime I shall continue to enjoy my study of the stars with my friends in the Doncaster Astronomical Society. I shall wonder at the awesome immensity and beauty of the universe. I shall be reminded of the words of the psalmist:

> *"When I consider thy heavens, the work of thy fingers, the moon and the stars, which thou hast ordained; what is man, that thou art mindful of him? And the son of man, that thou visitest him?"[112]*

---

[111] William Lane Craig: "Cosmology," in (Ed) Hastings, Mason and Pyper: **The Oxford Companion to Christian Thought,** O.U.P. 2000

[112] First Published in *Church and Community*, September 2003

Religion

Not religious

Sitting in a jacuzzi at the Dome (a modern futuristic designed leisure centre near Doncaster) yesterday, lazing on a bed at the side of the Oasis pool, and observing the delight of the children emerging from the shute, I found myself in sympathy with all those seekers after pleasure who have found inspiration in the teaching of that ancient philosopher Epicurus who taught that pleasure was the chief end of human life. Sipping a cappuccino in the café afterwards, however, my thoughts moved on from hedonism to theology, and I reflected that most of my fellow pleasure seekers probably managed their lives quite comfortably without any need to think of God, or indeed to consider his meaning and existence.

Religion is a funny thing, isn't it? Most of us are able to live without it, thank God, for most of the time; yet when calamities threaten, like war, or personal illness, or the death of a friend, then the uncertainties, what the philosophers call the existential questions, return. Why does it happen? Why evil? Why pain and suffering? Within these questions, is there God? The flickering answers which we struggle to find to these problems, which have been with mankind since as long as there has been human thought, range from a confident atheism (there is no God), through agnosticism (I cannot make up my mind) to faith (even though Thou slay me, I will adore Thee). So some of us turn to religion seeking answers and assurance, looking for a peace to calm our troubled spirits. For the symbol of our parish church building, bits of which have been here since the Normans and much of which will outlive us all (can stones live?), is a powerful reminder both of our historical inheritance and of the transitoriness and arbitrariness of our lives.

Religion is a funny thing because it provides no ultimate solace and no unequivocal answer to our agonising search for meaning and purpose in life. Bonhoeffer, you recall, wrote of religionless Christianity,[113] and he was a Christian minister, and probably a saint too. Therefore, we need to distinguish between religion (doing the things that busy church people often do) and Christianity that although it embraces religious activities, is fundamentally and radically different. Now if you have been kind enough to follow my argument thus far, I would like to invite you to consider this Easter thought: the way of Jesus Christ is not about being *religious* (e.g. saying prayers, being good, not being too unkind about one's neighbours, giving to the needy etc.) but about taking up a cross. The way of the cross contains a contradiction, for first it means following a person who says that the way to God is discerned neither in the power structures of the world, nor in the arrogant and the complacent, but in the powerless, the poor, the meek and the humble; and second, it means that this way leads to ultimate joy and peace. The contradiction, of course, is that the latter only comes through the former.

---

[113] Bonhoeffer Dietrich: **Letters and Papers from Prison: The Enlarged Edition,** SCM Press 1971

Not Religious

"Experience is not what happens to a man: it's what he does with what happens to him," wrote Aldous Huxley. Therefore, if we have already a faith in God or if we haven't, it's what we <u>do</u> with it, which is important. In other words, it is the way we live – our values as well as our prejudices, our hopes and our fears, our generosity as well as our lack of it – that counts.

If we look carefully at the life of the churches in our village, (and by this I mean the life, not just what goes on in the buildings) we shall discover that there is much *religious* activity going on (some people go to the Dome, others to church, and some to both), but also in the middle of it all, sometimes obviously so, but sometimes more difficult to find, there are unmistakable signs of real Christianity.[114]

---

[114] First Published in **Church and Community**, April 1991

Dimensions of Religion

According to the new Agreed Syllabus for Religious Instruction to be followed in Doncaster schools from next September 1985,[115] the study of religion involves seven dimensions. These dimensions provide a valuable basis for organising the religious education curriculum in schools and can be applied to the study of any major religion – Hinduism, Sikhism, Buddhism, Islam, Christianity. At a time of congregational introspection when Methodists are welcoming their new minister and when Anglicans are going into retreat at Whirlow Grange[116] these seven dimensions suggest pertinent questions for an understanding of our local churches, their nature and purpose both within the total religious context of Christianity and within the enveloping secular culture of our village and national life.

The first three dimensions are unproblematic – the social, ritual and experiential. Ninian Smart in his book *Secular Education and the Logic of Religion*[117] has named these dimensions as *historical*, that is, they are open to inspection and can be described and understood using the same language and analytic tools which we apply to other aspects of human culture. The sort of questions then are: how are our churches organised, what kinds of worship and ritual do we use, and how do individual members perceive, describe and live their religious

---

[115] Published by **Doncaster Local Education Authority**, 1984.
[116] Whirlow Grange is an Anglican Retreat Centre near Sheffield
[117] Ninian Smart: **Secular Education and the Logic of Religion**, Faber 1968

experience of God? There are differences here between our two congregations. We all know, however, that there are some experiences and perceptions which we share in common, for example, our delight in celebrating the great Christian festivals of Christmas and Easter, our love of the great Wesley hymns, and our acceptance of the authority of an ordained minister for defining matters of church order and worship.

The next three dimensions, matters of doctrine, myth and ethics, are also of crucial importance for understanding our churches. Smart argues that we cannot separate these *parahistorical* questions from the *historical* aspects of a religion. Indeed, the *parahistorical* can only be seen and understood in relation to them. To omit the *parahistorical* would be seriously to distort the nature of religion. Hence, to understand our Sprotbrough churches, we need to reflect carefully not only on our social, ritual and experiential existences but also on the beliefs, stories and values that are of major and central importance to us. I guess that when we do consider these issues carefully, we shall emphasise three things, namely, the doctrine of grace, the significance of Jesus, and Christian behaviour.

First, the doctrine of grace – the belief that when we start to look for God we discover to our astonishment that God has already found us! This truth is conveyed powerfully in many of the hymns of Charles

Wesley and in the popular hymn "Amazing Grace". As the writer of the letter to the Ephesians says: "*By grace ye are saved through faith*".[118]

Second, the significance of the central story for Christians of a man born in poverty who lived in historical obscurity, was executed as a criminal, and who rose from the dead. What impact does the story of Jesus make on our lives?

Third, the conviction that an adequate moral response to the figure and person of Jesus is to work out in the twentieth century appropriate individual and corporate responses to issues of poverty, unemployment, racism, apartheid, injustice and war.

The seventh dimension is the personal one: it is the assumption that religion is about personal identity, human nature, the human condition and the possibility of purpose in life. Religion amongst other philosophies raises questions and provides some possible answers and responses. To ask questions about ourselves, our loves and our hates, our values and our beliefs, our hopes and our fears, our convictions and our uncertainties – is also a valid approach to religious understanding.

My wish for both our congregations, therefore, is that we should learn to delight in the multi-faceted nature of our religion and that we should study it in all its dimensions.

---

[118] Ephesians 2: 8-9

I know that this letter is read by many people who do not have formal contact with our congregations. If you have been kind enough to read this far, and if perhaps you see yourself as an interested and sometimes bemused observer of the religious activity of this village, may I address a personal word to you? The argument of this letter is plain: it is that religion is an exciting human enterprise. You will find within our congregations a warm welcome, kindness and friendship, and above all tolerance. You will find those with a firm and strong faith in God; and you will find those for whom religion is a developing experience of a journey into self-understanding. Please come and join us.[119]

---

[119] First Published in *Church and Community*, August 1985

The Language of Religion

The other day I was walking down a road in the centre of Doncaster called Wood Street. A weary workman was leaning against the wall taking a short rest. Directly above him there was a Wayside Pulpit notice that read: *Every virtuous act is a step towards God.* I pointed this out to the workman who asked with some astonishment: "What does it mean?"

I was reminded of another conversation recently with a colleague at College. *"By your fruits ye shall know them"*, I had remarked. "Yes", she said, "But would you please explain to me what it means?"

People's puzzlement with the use of religious language is described in many places in the Bible. For instance, Nicodemus who came to Jesus by night, and the lawyer who asked "Who is my neighbour?", and the Pharisees who grumbled because Jesus spent his time with people of doubtful character. To Nicodemus Jesus spoke about spiritual birth,[120] to the lawyer he told the parable of the Good Samaritan,[121] and to the Pharisees he spoke about the Lost Son.[122] As to the question of religious people getting mixed up in politics, Jesus spoke those memorable words: *"Render to Caesar the things which are Caesar's and to God the things which are God's"*. [123]

---

[120] John 3, 5.
[121] Luke 10, 30.
[122] Luke 15, 11.
[123] Mark 12, 17.

The Language of Religion

There is a danger that when we discover people's genuine bafflement with religious words and phrases we respond by over simplification or trivialisation. We must avoid what a friend of mine calls sound-bite religion. Instead, in private conversation and in public worship our aim should be to expound the great Christian doctrines which underpin our faith, whilst using words which people understand and in ways to which people can respond with integrity.[124]

---

[123] Mark 12, 17.
[124] First Published in *Church and Community*, May 1997

Loneliness

The other lunch-time I sat down next to a student in the refectory who was sitting at a table by herself. "Are you lonely" I enquired. "Alone but not lonely" was her quick reply.

Bonhoeffer would have approved of her reply. "Let him who is afraid to be alone beware of being in the company of others" he once wrote. We need privacy, space, solitude – so that when we are in the company of others we can relate to them positively, with sensitivity and understanding. Dom Bede Griffiths, a Benedictine monk, whom I once had the privilege of meeting, and who has spent the last 35 years living a life of simplicity in an Ashram in South India, said recently: "Everyone needs an inner space". Then taking that beautiful Indian symbol of the lotus flower, he continued, "Just as there is a space at the heart of the lotus, so each of us needs an inner space to develop our own spirituality, our own being".[125]

Yes, each of us needs to find times when we can be alone, for such times will provide us with opportunities to discover that inner peace and serenity that enables us to live creatively when we return into the company of others. When we are alone, like Elijah in the cave on the mountainside, there is the possibility of hearing "the sound of a

---

[125] See – Judson Trapnell: **Bede Griffiths: A Life in Dialogue,** State University of New York Press, 2001

crushed silence".[126]   It is said that at the centre of a whirlpool there is a place of utmost calm where even a baby could lie unharmed.   In solitude too there is always the possibility of hearing God speaking to us: "*What doest thou here, Elijah?*" If within the silence there is a question, or a summons, we shall find too the compulsion to return into the company of others.

Alone but not lonely. I doubt whether my student friend realised neither how profound her utterance was nor what theological significance I would attach to it!   However, what of lonely people, really lonely people? They are around us all the time. We meet them in the crowd in the pub, in the classroom, in the shop, on the bus, and even at home. For loneliness describes not only those who are isolated by sickness, age and infirmity but also those who for a variety of reasons seem incapable of relating to other people. Such a failure to communicate leaves them feeling unwanted, unloved and truly alone. Lonely people are found most often, not by themselves, but in the company of others. All of us need each other as much as we need the air which we breathe.

May I ask you therefore, if you have followed my argument so far, to do two things. (1) Find time to be alone. (2) Find time to respond to those who need you. Let us be alert to the lonely in our midst. Let us

---

[126] This is a literal translation of the Hebrew in **1 Kings 19 v 12** which is sometimes translated "*a still small voice*".

respect each other's need for inner space and privacy, but let us offer conversation, hospitality and friendship to people who need us.[127]

---

[127] First Published in *Church and Community*, March 1988

Religious Education

Religious education is in the news and the Government appears to be on the verge of taking a backward step by introducing legislation[128] that will require that religious education in schools should be predominantly about the teaching of Christianity. Before we shout "Hurray for the Bishop of London and Baroness Cox" let us pause for a minute and consider what the aims and method of religious education in our schools should be.

wife of my late st Catherine's friend Murray Cox.

The aims of religious education:

1. to invite children to explore the nature and diversity of religion – its beliefs, ethics, stories, rituals, experience and organisations
2. to develop sensitivity, understanding and tolerance towards those of other faiths and philosophies of life
3. to help children to understand what is at the heart of religion, namely, an openness to the possibility of the discovery of the transcendent – what a famous theologian once called the idea of the holy[129]
4. to equip children with skills to practise the religious life, that is, how to meditate, how to be absolutely still, how to pray, how to worship
5. to develop appropriate attitudes, skills and concepts with regard to religion so that children may make their own choices of a faith to live by

The method of religious education:

---

[128] **Education Reform Act**, 1988
[129] Otto R: **The Idea of the Holy**, Oxford University Press, 1950

1. should provide an atmosphere in the classroom which is "open and critical" and which shows respect, sympathy, tolerance and understanding towards people of all faiths
2. must avoid indoctrination. Beliefs should be taught as beliefs within the context of particular religious traditions and the plurality of beliefs in contemporary society should be recognised and respected
3. must be related to the particular stage of emotional and cognitive development of children. Hence great care must be taken by the teacher in choosing material which is within the range of comprehension of the pupils

I believe, therefore, that to restrict religious education in our day schools to the teaching of only Christianity would be a backward step.[130]

---

[130] First Published in *Church and Community*, August 1988

Theology

Faith with a Bit of Doubt

One Sunday morning in the town of Heath, Massachusetts, American Supreme Court Justice Felix Frankfurter stopped on the way out of the little chapel to shake hands with the minister: "I liked what you said, Minister, and I speak as a believing unbeliever". "I'm glad you did, the minister answered, "For I spoke as an unbelieving believer".

The point of this story which I have quoted from a book *Faith without Religion*[131] is that the opposite of faith is not unbelief but disbelief. The unbeliever is not entirely lacking in faith, for despite his doubts, he does believe but recognizes his need to believe with more conviction and intensity. Many of us are surely in that position: we know that we need *"to believe more"*. Quite frankly, faith with a bit of doubt is a very reasonable position to be in. It places us alongside those who are searching, seeking, learning and exploring. We are rightly suspicious of know-alls. Although the Christian Church invites us to put our trust unequivocally in Jesus Christ it is also the case that faith has to be both nurtured and renewed: it is a continuous process. "Lord I believe: help thou my unbelief." There are certainly some serious objections which can be made against Christian belief – philosophical, psychological, moral? But equally, a strong case can be made in its favour. For my part, I find materialism, atheism and agnosticism fail to satisfy where I need most help. They are tenable intellectual positions to hold when

---

[131] Brown, Fred: **Faith without religion**, SCM, 1971

all is well. But they provide me with no comfort or sustenance when the going gets rough. All of us (dare I make a dogmatic assertion?), need the comfort and strength which a religious view of life (searching, seeking, finding, loving, worshipping, serving) can provide.

An Indian child blind from birth was given a simple eye operation that restored her sight. As the bandages were removed she was seen stretching out her hands trying to catch and hold the light in her outstretched hands. That's just what it is like to be an unbelieving believer – reaching out, and upwards towards the possibility of God, trying to grasp in part what can never be grasped in total. Talking of God – is it a coincidence that in my experience the Indian villager with the minimum of personal possessions, living on the edge of sudden unemployment, disease, hunger, and death often has a much stronger belief in the reality of God than does the sophisticated, modern, affluent and educated Englishman? Is our secularity and material wealth a hindrance to belief? Most of the time, we in the west, succeed in managing our lives quite well without God – or so it might seem. Such a position, however, does not dispose of the idea of God. On the contrary, according to Bonhoeffer, the God who lets us live in the world without the working hypothesis of God[132] is the God before whom we stand continually. That is – our belief (and unbelief) is one thing; the reality of God is another.[133]

---

[132] Bonhoeffer, **Letters and Papers**, op cit
[133] First Published in *Church and Community*, May 1984

Why should this happen to me?

The recent BBC television drama documentary *Threads*[134] was a frightening and disturbing experience. It provided a dramatic account of a nuclear holocaust and its effect on the city of Sheffield showing the eventual long run effects of nuclear war on civilization. People with whom I have spoken have confirmed a similar reaction to the film. Like *The Day After*[135] one was left with an overwhelming sense of despair and with a conviction of the evil, futility and absurdity of nuclear war. Despair, however, is an entirely negative reaction and other things need to be said and reflected upon.

Whatever our political conviction and loyalty, all of us must be united to work towards a reduction of the threat of nuclear war. That means that we must work within the political structures of our society putting influence and pressure where it will be most effective. We recognise, as Christians, that God has given us responsibility for our world. We recognise also, that God does not interfere in the natural processes of the world and if man chooses to destroy himself through nuclear war God will not intervene. *Threads* dramatically raises the theological problem of God and evil.

---

[134] Threads was a TV film created by the BBC, first shown in 1984 and repeated in 1985 as part of a week of programmes to commemorate the 40th anniversary of the atom bomb attacks on Japan.
[135] An ABC film, first shown in 1983, about the weeks leading up to and following a nuclear attack on the USA.

All of us have experienced situations of personal tragedy and sorrow, or at least we know people who have endured suffering and loss. In such experiences our common human reaction has been to ask the question why. Why should this happen to me? What have I done to deserve this fate? Why? Has it been our experience that when we have found no answer we have felt bitter and angry? Some of you reading these words will know exactly what I mean. I wish to say to you that the absence of any divine influence in our perception of the situation does not mean that God is not there. Indeed, on the contrary, I believe that God is often nearest when we perceive him to be farthest away! Christian faith is not the belief that God can remove suffering and evil, but that God permits both because he is love. A Christian pastor and theologian has written that:

> We may not understand why God permits suffering and evil but if, through Jesus Christ, we have a glimmer of understanding of what it means to say God is love, that why? will be hidden in light rather than in darkness.

To believe that God permits evil because he is love is no easy doctrine but it is the Christian's alternative to despair. Neither is it trite; nor is it easy to assert. Only one who has understood what it means to be cast into outer darkness can rejoice because Light has come into the world. Faith in God's care is an unconditional trust in his sovereignty even in relation to evil. Nothing can separate us from God's love, not evil, not pain, not suffering, not death. There is nothing that can force itself between God's love and the man of faith. There is absolutely nothing that evil can do to prevent that reality. This applies to all our pains and agonies now as well as in the future. As Charles Wesley wrote:

As far from danger as from fear,
While love, almighty love, is near.[136]

---

[136] First Published in **Church and Community**, November 1984

Perceptions of Self

My reading difficulties were increasing and something had to be done urgently. To grasp the intricate detail of the print successfully it was necessary to hold my glasses further and further down the nose; clearly a visit to my optician was imperative. As always, he was reassuring but told me something that I had never quite grasped 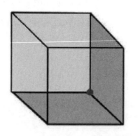 before – I was long-sighted and theoretically the focal point of my vision was infinity. It was the close at hand which was the problem; distances could be coped with.

A favourite problem which I enjoy discussing with students is the Necker Cube.[137] It is a vivid reminder of the multi-dimensionality of perception. As we look at it, first our eyes focus on the front and then on the back; suddenly we see one cube and then just as quickly the perspective changes and we see another. Things, it seems, are not what they appear to be. "Reality" said Picasso, "is more than the thing itself. I always look for its super-reality. Reality lies in how you see things. A green parrot is a green salad and a green parrot. He who

---

[137] Discovered in 1832 by the Swiss crystallographer L. A. Necker; this ambiguous picture now bears his name. The wire frame cube depicted in the *orthographic projection*, loses perspective clues that would otherwise help the brain identify the cube's orientation.

makes it only a parrot diminishes its reality." When a lady looking at a picture in Matisse's studio remarked, "Surely the arm of this woman is much too long" the artist replied, "Madam, you are mistaken. This is not a woman. This is a picture."

How reliable is our perception when we look at ourselves? Most likely we shall get a distorted view, and even then how can we be certain that what we see is reality – is really me? Perhaps we can cope with looking at others, in the distance as it were, and maybe like my eye-sight condition, the real difficulty lies with the close at hand? If we dare risk a measure of introspection what are we to do with the fears, guilts, uncertainties and inconsistencies which, if Freud is right, we shall find? Or if we take a more optimistic view of human nature and its potential, will we nevertheless find an overwhelming desire for security and safety which prevents us from taking risks, breaking old habits, and addressing the future courageously? Will we find ourselves imprisoned by different layers of circumstances that do not allow us to step out and take responsibility for our lives? I suspect that because perception is itself a very elaborate psychological process, there are no quick and obvious answers to my questions. There is value, nevertheless, in pondering them, and I would like to hazard a guess that some of the answers can only be found in the company of others. Perception of self involves in part the perception of self through the eyes of other people.[138]

---

[138] First Published in **Church and Community**, March, 1985

Good Friday

An atheist friend of mine went into a church recently to listen to his daughter play in an orchestral service. "I had not been in a church for twenty years," he said, "and I was astonished at the doctrine which I heard". In fact, from his atheistic intellectual position he was somewhat appalled. I wonder whether you feel scandalised or offended by the doctrine of the cross that the church celebrates at this time of year? Yes, celebrates is the right word here. For Christianity is about believing and celebrating the reality of God revealed in the cross of Christ.

"Christ died: it is for man to discern the doctrine" said Whitehead. What do we discern? We see the cruelty and barbarity of men; we see courage in the face of death; we see friends deserting when their loyalty is needed; we see the grief and distress of a mother. All these human behaviours are recorded in the Good Friday story, and we identify their authentic validity because they are experiences that we encounter in our lives today. There are other experiences there too if we are prepared to probe deeply, *parahistorical* factors, one theologian has called them. We see despair, agony, loneliness, and deep ache of the heart caused by loss of meaning, when despite the love of friends and the care of relatives the future is empty and bleak. "My God, my God, why hast thou forsaken me?" cried Jesus. That is a twentieth century cry in the prisons, hospitals, and refugee camps of our contemporary world. It is the cry of the hungry and the dispossessed; it is our cry too.   It is within these experiences that create self-doubt and despair that God comes to us.

> *"Pain that cannot forget*
> *Falls drop by drop upon the heart*
> *Until in our despair*
> *There comes wisdom*
> *Through the awful grace of God."*

The miracle of the cross is that it enables us to discover the meaning of God being present in our unique and individual situations. It is the sense of being astonished by grace and of being amazed and overwhelmed by love. It means that in the blackness of the tunnel we glimpse the light coming towards us. It means that each of us can find a way to reconciliation, to forgiveness, to peace and to hope.[139]

---

[139] First Published in **Church and Community**, March 1986

Easter

One of the formative influences on my life is the late Reverend Frederic Greeves. He was principal of my theological college in Bristol where I was trained for the ministry and I owe an immense debt to him. He was a saintly person, a deep thinker, a theologian and psychologist. If I were to describe him, I would wish to portray those attributes in that order of importance. Although he once said to me that he did not regard himself as a scholar, the University of Bristol awarded him an honorary Doctorate of Laws, and in 1963 he was President of the Methodist Conference. He published two major books, one was entitled: *The Meaning of Sin*, and the other *Theology and the Cure of Souls*.

In College chapel he would always sit at the back and the rumour was that he would never fail to notice if anyone was absent! I remember he once said: "The times when you least feel like going to chapel, are precisely the times when you most need to be there". Another of his stories was about the woman he once approached about confirmation. "My dear Mr Greeves," she said, 'If you would like me to be a church member, of course I will be confirmed!" "No madam", he briskly replied, "when you realise what a privilege it is to belong to God's people, and when you know how much you need to experience that privilege, then, and not until then, let us talk about your membership!" As I reflect upon his influence, I realise that most of all, within the deep quietness and serenity of his personality he communicated a genuine sincerity and conviction of Christian faith. Like that giant of a theologian, Karl Barth, he believed that faith was quite simply a gift from God, not deserved, not achieved, not the result of merit of good works, but a gracious gift from Almighty God.

By the time you read this, Easter will be almost upon us. Easter Day symbolises the creation of the Christian Church, and it all began with ordinary people, like ourselves, discovering a faith in God which was centred in the enigma of a man called Jesus. The earliest appearances of Jesus were met with incredulity. The Easter stories in the Bible depict people who were full of fear, doubt and uncertainty. Yet the doubt and fear struggled with joy and worship. They described the experience as having "seen the Lord". Those early descriptions of Christian experience are primarily about faith, joy, and hope!

I know that some of you reading this, from your own recent personal circumstances will easily identify with the situation of those early first century Christian believers. Mary weeping in the garden overwhelmed with her personal grief. Thomas doubting the possibility of faith. The travellers on the road to Emmaus pondering over the meaning of crucifixion and unable to experience the joy and hope which lay beyond it. The women fleeing the tomb with amazement and fear. Saul on the Damascus road, "Who art thou Lord?"

Is it possible that you desire faith but have not found it? Perhaps your world is so full of personal worries that even the possibility of an encounter with the living Lord seems unthinkable? Remember then, faith is a gift from God. What is needed is our willingness to listen, and to be ready to receive it.

> *Almighty and everlasting God, increase in us your gift of faith, that forsaking what lies behind and reaching out to that which is before, we may run the way of your commandments and win the crown of everlasting joy, through Jesus Christ our Lord. Amen.*[140]

---

[140] First Published in ***Church and Community***, April 1994

Something to Boil

The other day I travelled up to London. It's fun travelling on the inter-city 125; it's fast and one soon gets there. Travelling is exciting because we pass through strange places that we have never visited before. We catch a fleeting glimpse and they are gone. We view from our carriage window strangers going about their daily business, lorry drivers, children on their way to school, women pegging washing on a line.   But these observations from the train are merely fleeting perceptions of our common humanity, forgotten as soon as they are seen! For the traveller's main preoccupation is the business of the journey and the nature of the destination at which he will soon arrive.

The metaphor of the journey is a vivid description of Christianity. Christians are pilgrims of no fixed abode. Like the Hebrews of old we are moving onwards to the Promised Land. Our hope is in God who is always with us on our journey and ahead of us ready to welcome us at our destination. If this is a true description of Christianity, then it describes our churches in this village, or at least, it describes our churches how they might be. Our characteristic lifestyle is one of change, movement, creativity, experiment, dissatisfaction with the present – and always openness to the future.

This kind of faith, moreover, is not a flight from the world; it is not other-worldly. The church is the company of those people who here and now try to live, believe, love and hope in terms of God's promised future. Christian hope is not a quietist expectation like sitting around in a waiting room till God opens the door of his office! Only those who seek find; and the door is opened only to those who knock. We are builders of the future, whose power, in hope as well as in fulfilment, is God. The writer Ernst Bloch suggested that Christian hope "is not only something to drink but also something to boil". In other words, Christian hope is not something that just happens to us; rather it is an active grasping of the reality of God who meets us in Jesus Christ. The church is not the goal of its own movement; the goal is the Kingdom of God, the world redeemed.[141]

Two things follow from these remarks. (1) Our churches could pay a self-critical glance at their structures and ethos. They could usefully consider whether their priorities are about change and movement or whether they are more concerned at preserving the *status quo*. (2) Individually we can re-affirm our faith in God through Jesus Christ who summons us into the unknown future, who travels with us, and who welcomes us at each new stage of the journey.[142] [143]

---

[141] J. Moltmann, "The future as threat and as opportunity", D R Cutler (Ed.): **The World Year Book of Religion**, Volume II, Evans 1969

[142] See Jehuda Hallevie: "*As I set off on my way to You, I found You coming toward me*". (quoted by Moltmann, loc. cit.)

[143] First Published in **Church and Community**, November 1987

Lessing's Question

Some time in the 1920s, in South India, a man picked up a gospel booklet in the local market and began to read. He was so enthralled by the story of Jesus Christ that he invited the local missionary in Dharapuram[144] to visit his village. Following the missionary's visit and after some instruction the whole village received baptism and the mass movement of hundreds of villages converting to Christianity had begun. The history of the growth of Christianity in India is a story of mass movements in many parts of the country. During the 1960s when I was working in Dharapuram the distribution of tracts and gospels was a well-established method of evangelism. The conviction that the good news of Jesus Christ was for everyone, and had to be shared, was widespread throughout the Church.

As I look back on my ministry in the Church of South India I remember an occasion when we set up a small rostrum in a Hindu street in the predominantly Hindu town of Thanjavur[145] when I preached on the text: *"Jesus is the Way, the Truth and the Life"*. A Hindu gentleman approached me in genuine puzzlement. "Why are you giving this message in a Hindu street?" he asked. Simply distributing tracts, and preaching, were seen to be lacking in sophistication. Further dialogue was needed. Indeed it is interesting to note that the

---

[144] This is the town in Tamil Nadu, South India, where I was ordained Presbyter in the Church of South India on 12th March 1961

[145] I was Presbyter in Charge of St Peter's Church, Thanjavur from 1965 to 1969

first Indians to engage in Hindu-Christian dialogue were not Indian Christians but Indian Hindus of the reform movement Brahmo Samraj. For example, Rajah Rammohun Roy (1772-1833) who sought to provide innovative ways of interpreting Christ. Christian theology in India has developed considerably, however, since those early days when I served there as a missionary.

> *"Indian Christian thought today can be classified in two overarching clusters: religio-cultural, which takes India's spiritual and philosophic heritage seriously, and socio-political which focuses on inequalities and seeks liberation from oppressive social structures."[146]*

The question arises regarding what form of evangelism is appropriate in Britain for today? Maybe the distribution of tracts is the answer but I doubt it. Inviting people to view a video of the life of Christ is a similar method. The Alpha Project[147] is a method that is meeting with considerable success at the present time and many people have joined the Christian Church as a result of it. The aim is to invite people to consider the claims of Jesus Christ seriously. However, what is the best way to do this?

The clear message of the Gospel is that Jesus Christ is good news for all people, in all occupations, in all places and for all times. What does this mean in our day to day life? How is Jesus Christ to become relevant to the lives of our friends and neighbours including the people

---

[146] Sugirtharajah R. S: *Indian Christian Thought,* in (Ed.) Hastings A et al: **The Oxford Companion to Christian Thought**, Oxford University Press, 2000, page 324

[147] **The Alpha Course** originated at Holy Trinity Brompton, London in 1977 and since 1990 under the leadership of an Anglican Priest, the Reverend Nicky Gumbel has developed into a hugely successful world wide organisation for evangelism. See the Alpha Web Site at **http://alphacourse.org**

whose lives have been shattered by tragedy or changed irrevocably by illness or bereavement? Or as a theologian asked: "How can the life of a man who lived nearly 2000 years ago have relevance or significance for my life today?"[148]   To invite others to consider the Christian faith seriously requires sensitivity, openness, and perhaps as indicated by the Hindu gentleman in Thanjavur, a measure of sophistication.   Indeed, the very survival of the Christian Church in Britain may depend on its capacity to respond to a society that is at times tolerant but often sceptical of its claims, by entering into fruitful dialogue at the intellectual[149], political[150] and social[151] levels. So in welcoming everyone into our Church communities, not only at worship but also at other meetings and activities, let us enter into dialogue – with humility as well as enthusiasm.[152]

---

[148] See *Lessing's question* in Diem H: **Dogmatics**, Oliver and Boyd, 1959, page 9
[149] See for example: Ward G: **The Postmodern God**, Blackwell, 1997
[150] See for example: Forrester D: **Christian Justice and Public Policy**, Cambridge University Press, 1997
[151] See for example: Milbank J: **Theology and Social Theory**, Blackwell, 1993
[152] First Published in **Church and Community**, August 2001

Sir, We Would See Jesus

In ancient times people believed that the gods remained in the places which they inhabited. A particular village would have its own god. When one went on a journey, therefore, one left one's god behind. It was a startling revelation to Jacob, on his journey, therefore, and in his dream, to discover that his god was still with him: "Surely the Lord is in this place and I knew it not".[153]   Moses too discovered that God was present with him, first in his spiritual encounter with God in the desert[154] and later in the events of the escape from Egypt and the journey in the wilderness.[155]

Imagine now the experience of the blind man who was begging at the side of the road in Jericho when Jesus and his disciples passed by. There was a huge crowd.   The noise of the excited shouting of the crowds almost drowned the sound of his voice.   He yelled: "Jesus, Jesus, have mercy upon me."   Would Jesus hear his voice? Would Jesus speak to him?   The story concludes that Jesus stood still and commanded that the man should be brought to him.[156]   Blind Bartimaeus received his sight.   To put it more poignantly, "Jesus stood still for one blind beggar in the dust".   I am reminded of a modern day story from India where a child who had received an eye

---

[153] Genesis 28 verse 16
[154] Exodus 3, verse 2
[155] Exodus 24, verse 15f
[156] Mark 10, verse 49

operation slowly unwound the bandages from her eyes. Suddenly she cried with joyful delight: "I see, I see!"

I have some vivid memories from India that haunt me still. I remember seeing a destitute child sleeping in the subway. I recall a man covered in rags dying on a roundabout as the traffic roared around him. I remember people with leprosy, beggars, pavement dwellers, and people who were hungry and starving. In our country social conditions are much better. Yet there are many people today (perhaps even <u>you</u> as you read this letter) who still desperately desire to discover the reality of the love, forgiveness and comfort of God in their lives.

St John's gospel contains deep theological reflection on the meaning of the life, death and resurrection of Jesus. There is one particular fragment,[157] however, which excites my attention and which illustrates the point I am trying to make in this article.[158] There were certain Greeks who wanted to see Jesus. They approached Jesus by speaking first to Philip and then to Andrew. It is not reported whether their request was granted. Instead there is a theological treatise which develops the view that the forthcoming crucifixion of Jesus will reveal God to all men. The episode ends curiously with Jesus hiding himself from the people.[159]

---

[157] John 12, verses 20-33
[158] *Note: I must avoid here the common pitfall of preachers who choose texts to illustrate their own thoughts!*
[159] John 12, verse 36

127

This passage in John's gospel is full of symbolism. We miss its meaning if we read it literally. The Greeks denote everyman. Everyman wishes to meet Jesus, and through Jesus everyman is offered an encounter with the living God. So, like the Greeks, if we would see Jesus, and through him find God, we must recognise that the way of Jesus is the way of the cross. We actually find God, through Jesus, in the midst of temptation, sin, pain, suffering, alienation, fear and despair. Maybe first, however, like blind Bartimaeus, we have to yell out, so that our cry is heard above the noise all around us.

I wonder why Jesus chose to hide himself. I wonder also whether the Greeks did indeed eventually meet Jesus? What do you think?[160]

---

[160] First Published in **Church and Community**, May 1998

A poem from South India

O God, who lives in the slums, where the sewage
runs down the back of the houses;
where the mud walls crumble when the monsoon comes;
where rain soaks through the holes in roofs —
Help us to know you.

O God, who crouches at church gates, where people
walk by after morning worship;
whose name is beggar, cripple, leper, pavement-dweller—
Help us to know you.

O God, who lives in the outcaste street, whose children
work to clear your debt;
who hungers because you are unemployed;
who despairs because children starve and women suffer—
Help us to know you.

O God, who lies down to die under the bridge in the city,
covered in a rag as the traffic roars by,
whose body is carted away by the municipal sweepers
because all have forsaken you—
Help us to know you.

O God, slum-dweller, beggar, cripple, leper—
O God, without work, hungry, thirsty—
O God, forsaken, alone—
Help us to know you.[161]

---

[161] First Published in *The Kingdom Overseas,* the magazine of the Methodist
Missionary Society; and in **The World Calls Christians to Prayer,** Cargate Press,
Methodist Church Overseas Division; and in Donald Hilton: **Liturgy of Life,**
National Christian Education Council, 1991, Reprinted 1992, 1995.

About the Author

Timothy Mark trained for the Methodist Ministry at Didsbury College, Bristol. After gaining a BA Honours in theology and a PGCE from Bristol University he went to St Andrew's College, Selly Oak, Birmingham for missionary training.

He was ordained in the Church of South India (deacon 1959, presbyter 1961) and was Manager and Correspondent of the CSI Boys' High School, Dharapuram (1962-64) and Presbyter-in-Charge of St Peter's Church, Thanjavur (1965-69). After returning to England he was Head of Religious Education at Passmores Comprehensive School, Harlow (1970-73) and on the staff of Doncaster College (1970-2000) lecturing in religious studies, education and psychology, and from 1990 until his retirement, was a member of the senior management team.

He married in 1975 Lorna Galloway who was a BEd student at Doncaster College of Education; they have two children, Kathryn and Richard. Lorna died in July 2000. Since retirement he has been the Education Officer for the Sheffield Methodist District Synod; he is also an active member of the Danum Social and Literary Society and of the Doncaster Astronomical Society.

Timothy was awarded three post-graduate degrees: MLitt (Bristol 1968), MEd (Bristol 1971) and PhD (Leeds 1979).

Original Dates of Publication

The letters were published in *The Church and Community in Sprotbrough* magazine in the following chronological sequence:

Letter	Published
Church Structures	Nov-82
The Church needs you	Mar-83
General Election 1983	Jun-83
Christmas: Light and Shadows	Dec-83
Faith with a Bit of Doubt	May-84
Why should this happen to me?	Nov-84
Perceptions of Self	Mar-85
Dimensions of Religion	Aug-85
Good Friday	Mar-86
Watch Night Service in India	Jan-87
General Election 1987	Jun-87
Something to Boil	Nov-87
Loneliness	Mar-88
Religious Education	Aug-88
New Year	Jan-89
Christianity and Politics	Jul-89
Responding To Christmas	Jan-90
Church Notice Boards	Jun-90
Not religious	Apr-91
Charismatic Christians	Sep-91
Christmas in Our Secular Community	Dec-91
General Election 1992	Apr-92
Not a Church Going Christian	Aug-92
The Dam Busters	Jun-93
Stories	Nov-93
Easter	Apr-94
Reading the Bible	Sep-94
Epiphany	Feb-95
Kafka's Parable	Aug-95
An Impromptu Sermon	Feb-96
The Old House	Aug-96
The Language of Religion	May-97
Mission	Nov-97

Original Dates Of Publication

Letter	Published
Sir, We Would See Jesus	May-98
Racism, Capitalism and Religious Belief	Nov-98
Secular Christmas	Feb-99
Millennium	Aug-99
How Can We Bridge The Gap?	Feb-01
Lessing's Question	Aug-01
Destruction of the Twin Towers	Sep-02
Let there be Light	Sep-03
Safe in the Last Homely House	Aug-04
Deep Impact and Deep Tragedy	Aug-05

Bibliography

Brown Fred: **Faith without religion**, SCM, 1971

Bonhoeffer D: **Letters and Papers from Prison,** Macmillan 1967

Bonhoeffer Dietrich: **Letters and Papers from Prison:** Enlarged Edition**,** SCM Press 1971

Bonhoeffer Dietrich: **The Cost of Discipleship**, Peter Smith, 1983

Browning Robert: **Men and Women,** J M Dent, 1939

Cummings E.E: **A Miscellany**, Harcourt Brace Jovanovich, Inc. 1955

Cutler D R (Ed.): **The World Year Book of Religion**, Volume II, Evans 1969

Diem H: **Dogmatics**, Oliver and Boyd, 1959

Donne John: **Devotions upon Emergent Occasions**, 1624

Eliot T S: **Collected Poems 1909-1935**, Faber, 1958.

Forrester D: **Christian Justice and Public Policy**, Cambridge University Press**,** 1997

Greene Brian: **The Fabric of the Cosmos**, Penguin, 2005

Gwatkin H M: **Selections from Early Christian Writers**, Macmillan 1920

Hastings, Mason and Pyper (Eds): **The Oxford Companion to Christian Thought,** O.U.P. 2000

Hilton Donald: **Liturgy of Life,** National Christian Education Council, 1991, Reprinted 1992, 1995.

James M & Jongeward D: **Born to Win**, Signet 1978

Kierkegaard Soren: **Fear and Trembling,** Penguin August 1985

Lopez Barry: **Crow and Weasel**, Ebury Press, 1991

Milbank J: **Theology and Social Theory**, Blackwell, 1993

Otto R: **The Idea of the Holy**, Oxford University Press, 1950

Richardson Alan: **An Introduction to the Theology of the New Testament**, SCM Press 1958

Rippin Bryan: **The Christian Juggler**, Epworth, 1985

Samarin W. J: **Tongues of Men and Angels: the Religious Language of Pentecostalism**, Collier Macmillan, 1972

Smart Ninian : **Secular Education and the Logic of Religion**, Faber 1968

Tolkien J R R: **The Lord of the Rings**, Harper Collins, 1991

Trapnell Judson**: Bede Griffiths: A Life in Dialogue,** State University of New York Press, 2001

The Kingdom Overseas, the magazine of the Methodist Missionary Society

The World Calls Christians to Prayer, Cargate Press, Methodist Church Overseas Division

Ward G: **The Postmodern God**, Blackwell, 1997

Index

Galileo, 87

God, ix, 3, 4, 5, 6, 8, 9, 11, 12, 13, 14, 16, 18, 19, 21, 22, 23, 24, 26, 27, 36, 41, 44, 46, 48, 50, 58, 65, 67, 70, 83, 88, 89, 93, 94, 95, 97, 99, 100, 101, 103, 110, 111, 112, 116, 117, 121, 122, 125, 129, 134

God the Holy Spirit, 51

Gordon Brown, 76, 82

grace, 12, 13, 14, 18, 23, 58, 97, 117

history, 11, 26, 31, 33, 123

Holy Communion, ix, 8

hope, 3, 19, 23, 25, 27, 33, 35, 65, 70, 117, 121, 122

horizons, 4, 48, 58

ideologies, 72, 82

India, ix, 3, 18, 23, 32, 40, 41, 45, 47, 81, 102, 123, 124, 129, 130

Jesus, 4, 9, 11, 13, 15, 17, 19, 25, 54, 55, 58, 59, 73, 94, 98, 100, 109, 112, 116, 119, 120, 122, 123, 124, 126, 127, 128

Jesus Christ, 4, 123, 124

Karl Barth, 13

Letter to Diognetus, 16

Local Ecumenical Partnership, 33

love, 18, 19, 24, 41, 44, 58, 68, 88, 97, 112, 113, 116, 117, 122

mission, 33, 34, 35, 45, 46, 47

Moral action,, 72

myth, 11, 15, 97

NASA, 84, 85

Ninian Smart, 96, 134

nuclear war, 111

perception, 112, 114, 115

personal tragedy, 21, 112

pilgrims, 14, 83, 121

poverty, 5, 16, 68, 98

Religion, 91, 93, 96, 98, 100, 109, 122, 133, 134

resurrection, 19

secular, ix, 11, 12, 14, 16, 17, 21, 35, 46, 67, 96

secular city, 14

secularity, 110

sound-bite religion, 101

South India, 41, 45, 123

speaking in tongues, 50

Steven Hawking, 88

strangers and foreigners, 14, 83

suffering, 3, 21, 23, 68, 82, 93, 112

suicide bombers, 81

terrorist attack, 85

The Bible, 58

The Church of South India, 32

the cross, 17, 48, 55, 59, 86, 94, 116, 117, 128,

The Day After, 111

The Lord of The Rings, 60, 134